"Beautiful and profound. With mystic vision and poetic clarity, Brother David opens us to the eternal vision behind the creed."

—Jack Kornfield, author of *The Wise Heart: A Guide to the Universal Teachings of Buddhist Psychology*

"There is only one Brother David! To be in his presence is to know the possibility of walking faithfully on one chosen path, while not only respecting other faiths, but also studying them rigorously and experiencing them joyfully. In *Deeper Than Words,* he distills a lifetime of insight into an inspiring book that can enlighten all of us to the universal similarities and the noble particularities of the world's wisdom traditions."

—Elizabeth Lesser, cofounder of Omega Institute and author of *The Seeker's Guide* and *Broken Open: How Difficult Times Can Help Us Grow*

"A stunning analysis. It may not make a believer out of you but it will show you the depth of meaning of the Apostles' Creed."

—Sam Keen, author of *In the Absence of God: Dwelling in the Presence of the Sacred*

"Faith is a journey of exhausting proportions that goes beyond the memorization of simple catechetics to the most profound of spiritual possibilities. It is that kind of faith of which this profoundly honest book speaks, a faith that lifts us all above the parochial and the sectarian to the spiritual heights at which we are all, indeed, One."

—Sister Joan Chittister, OSB, author of *The Gift of Years*

Deeper Than Words

Living the
Apostles' Creed

Brother David Steindl-Rast

IMAGE BOOKS / DOUBLEDAY
New York   London   Toronto   Sydney   Auckland

Published in the United States by Doubleday Religion,
an imprint of the Crown Publishing Group,
a division of Random House, Inc., New York.
www.crownpublishing.com
www.doubledayreligion.com

IMAGE, the Image colophon, and DOUBLEDAY are registered
trademarks of Random House, Inc.

"may i be gay," copyright © 1963, 1991 by the Trustees for the
E. E. Cummings Trust, from *Complete Poems: 1904–1962* by
E. E. Cummings, edited by George J. Firmage. Used by permission
of Liveright Publishing Corporation.

"My Papa's Waltz," copyright © 1942 by Hearst Magazines, Inc.,
from *Collected Poems of Theodore Roethke* by Theodore Roethke.
Used by permission of Doubleday, a division of Random House, Inc.

"On Thy Wondrous Works I Will Meditate (Psalm 145)" from *Thirst*
by Mary Oliver, published by Beacon Press in 2006, copyright © by
Mary Oliver. Used by permission of Mary Oliver.

"Trillium," copyright © by Patricia Campbell Carlson.
Used by permission.

"Yes" from *The Selected Poetry of Jessica Powers*. Published by
ICS Publications, Washington, D.C. All copyrights, Carmelite
Monastery, Pewaukee, Wisconsin. Used with permission.

All scripture quotations are the personal translations
of Brother David Steindl-Rast.

Library of Congress Cataloging-in-Publication Data
is available upon request.

ISBN 978-0-307-58961-3

PRINTED IN THE UNITED STATES OF AMERICA

Design by Donna Sinisgalli

1 3 5 7 9 10 8 6 4 2

First Edition

This book is dedicated to
you, my sisters and brothers,
who used to recite the Creed
but can no longer do so with honesty and conviction.
May it help you find new meaning in the words
and—deeper than words that divide—
the faith that unites all human beings.

———

With profound gratefulness,
I acknowledge the help of countless kind people
(far too many to list by name) who have made it
possible to conceive, to write, and to produce this
book and to put it into your, the reader's, hands
—and to you, the reader, for your interest.

Contents

Foreword by His Holiness the Dalai Lama

Wherever we live and whatever faith we uphold or none, we share the desire to live life to its fullest, to better ourselves and the lives of our loved ones. And wherever they originally arose, all the world's major religious traditions are similar in having the potential to help human beings live at peace with one another, with themselves, and with our natural environment.

I first really became aware that discussion between sincere practitioners of Christianity and Buddhism could be mutually enriching and spiritually sustaining for both parties when Thomas Merton came to see me many years ago. The courage he showed in exploring faith traditions beyond his own so that he could, as it were, taste the actual flavor of the teachings that other traditions represent opened my eyes. It was a source of real inspiration. Since then I have been fortunate to befriend other individuals whose joyful experience of faith in their own spiritual lives has helped them appreciate the value of other traditions, rather than the exclusive preciousness of their own. I have had the privilege not only of talking to these exhilarating men and women, but also of sharing their prayers and practice. Prominent among them is Brother David Steindl-Rast, known to many simply as Brother David, a seasoned Benedictine monk and veteran of active interreligious dialogue.

Therefore, it is a great personal pleasure to me to see this new book of Brother David's, a book that he and I talked about, reach the light of day. In it he explores how the Christian belief in Creation and the Buddhist understanding of Interdependent Arising are two different pointers toward the same experience. He demonstrates how it may be possible for someone to remain perfectly faithful to a Christian and Western monastic commitment and yet be enriched by, say, Buddhist understanding and experience. Of course, the same is true from the Buddhist side as well. Indeed, the essence of genuine interreligious dialogue must be founded on such a conviction.

The kind of courage I mentioned above is present again here in that Brother David has chosen as his text the Apostles' Creed, a fundamental expression of Christian faith. He approaches it by asking point by point, what does this mean? How do we know? And why is it important? The openhearted candor of his answers to these questions, reaching into his own living and contemporary experience, is what gives his words value and power. Brother David places great store by the marvelous unifying idea of gratefulness. Gratefulness for the kindness of the Creator and Creation resonates clearly with gratefulness for the kindness of the Buddha and all sentient beings. To nurture gratefulness in our hearts is to nurture a positive mind. And a positive mind is something that ultimately brings us benefit or happiness. I am sure many readers will join me in feeling grateful to Brother David for his kindness in writing this book.

February 2010

Deeper Than Words

"God Isn't Someone Else"

❧

Imagine a monastery perched on a high cliff overlooking the Danube River in Austria. Benedictine monks have worked and prayed in this place for nine hundred years without interruption. His Holiness the Dalai Lama spent three days here, joining us Benedictines simply as a monk among monks. He worshipped with us in the chapel at the hours of prayer and ate with us in the monastic refectory. It was during one of those meals that he turned to me and said somewhat abruptly, "We have so much in common, you and I, but one thing separates us: the idea of a divine Creator." This was a challenge, though not at all in the sense of a defiant confrontation. The Dalai Lama's voice expressed a genuine sadness over perceived disagreement, a pain that challenged my compassion. Four decades of participating in Buddhist/Christian dialogues had prepared me for all that came into focus at that moment. It was a challenge, I had to rise to it, and I did.

Don't ask me how. Firemen make split-second decisions at a crucial moment, rescue a life, and are unable afterward to tell how they did it. In a kind of improvised elevator speech, I had to do two things at once: stay true to my Christian tradition's belief in Divine Creation and show that it was compatible with Buddhist belief in Interdependent Arising. It all hinged on bridging the gap between Creator and creation, a gap that is merely speculative and not grounded in experience. After all, the late Thomas Merton, Trappist monk and friend of both the Dalai Lama and myself, had been able to crystallize the key insight into a four-word sentence: "God isn't someone else." For the mystic there is no gap between Creator and creation. The whole universe is an expression of divine life.

The cosmic web of mutually interdependent cause and effect in which all things arise is what the mystic poet Kabir sees as "the Secret One slowly growing a body."

Thus, belief in Creation and belief in Interdependent Arising are two different expressions of one and the same underlying faith—two different pointers toward the same experience. Faith as experience lies deeper than words and concepts. It is an inner gesture by which we entrust ourselves totally and unconditionally to life—life perceived as our own, yet as a power greater than ourselves.

The Dalai Lama beamed. "You must write about this," he urged me. "Gladly," I replied, "if Your Holiness will write the foreword"; and he agreed to do so. Now, I beamed.

In interreligious dialogue we tend to quote from our respective traditions those passages that the others are most likely to find acceptable. But increasingly this had begun to seem a bit superficial to me. I had come to feel that for genuine agreement we would have to go deeper; we would have to test whether even the least likely texts—say, a creed—could help deepen interreligious understanding. Wars have been fought even among co-religionists over these succinct summaries of essential beliefs. A creed would thus make the perfect touchstone for the possibility of interreligious agreement on that deep level where it matters. That's why I chose the Apostles' Creed—the oldest of the Christian creeds—and thus this book came about.

The creed expresses basic human faith in Christian terms, just as Buddhists' beliefs are an expression of that same basic human faith common to all. Faith—courageous trust in the mystery of Life—makes us human; and each culture, each period of history, gives this faith new expressions in beliefs that are determined by historic and cultural circumstances. Beliefs divide, but the faith from which they spring is one and unites. The task of interreligious dialogue is to make our divergent beliefs transparent to the one faith we share.

In this book I have tried to apply this principle to the Apostles'

Creed, a summary of the beliefs through which Christians profess their faith at Baptism. Taking its statements one by one, I have applied a three-pronged tool to each of them, asking three decisive questions. By asking, "What does this really mean?" I try to pry open the hard shell of preconceived notions that tends to form around set expressions we hear or use too often. Once this shell is cracked and you know what you mean, I ask, "How do you know?"—how do you personally know that this statement is true? This question no longer allows us to juggle with concepts, but forces us to link them with experience—yours, the reader's—since experience is the basis for genuine knowing. Finally I ask, "Why is this so important?"— important enough to be part of as succinct a document as the Creed, important therefore to the one who recites the Creed. (You will notice that these three questions get progressively more personal. Faith, together with the beliefs that express that faith, is a most personal concern, or it is not faith at all.) My What? How? Why? (to which I add brief personal reflections of my own) give this book its format.

Deep inner peace, a sense of belonging, and a firm anchorage in the eternal Now of the present moment, these are among the fruits that struggling humans throughout the centuries have reaped from the faith expressed in the Creed. I speak as a Christian who has prayed that Creed for almost eighty years, and I can vouch for it: these spiritual fruits are still available to us today as fresh as they ever were. Whether or not one holds the particular beliefs expressed in the Creed, anyone using my three-pronged tool should be able to recognize them as valid expressions of the faith that unites us as humans. I have tried to trigger that recognition. You, the reader, will have to judge whether I succeeded.

THE APOSTLES' CREED

I believe in **God**,
the Father Almighty,
the Creator of heaven and earth,

and in **Jesus Christ**,
God's only Son,
our Lord:

Who was conceived by the **Holy Spirit**,
born of the Virgin Mary,
suffered under Pontius Pilate,

was crucified,
died,
and was buried.
He descended into hell.

The third day He arose again from the dead.
He ascended into heaven
and sits at the right hand of God the Father Almighty,
thence He shall come to judge the living and the dead.

I believe in the **Holy Spirit**,

the holy catholic church,
the communion of saints,
the forgiveness of sins,
the resurrection of the body,
and life everlasting

Amen.

I Believe

～

What does this really mean?

The original version of the Creed begins with the word *credo*, from which the English word *creed* derives. The single word *credo* is translated by two English words, I BELIEVE. We shall take a closer look at the Latin word in the next section. Here we focus on the meaning of the "I" that speaks in the Creed. Who is that "I"?

Only when they are joined together in the phrase I BELIEVE do these two words reveal their full meaning. They define each other, as it were. When the "I" that speaks here "believes," this means infinitely more than accepting an unproven proposition as likely; it is rather an expression of unconditional trust. Only when we know that this is what believing means can we understand which "I" is speaking here; and only this "I," in turn, can believe, in the full sense of believing. Only an "I" brave enough for the radical confidence of unconditional trust can be our true Self. Our little ego—which we often mean when we say "I"—is incapable of the courageous trust of faith. Why? Because the opposite of faith as trust is not doubt but fearfulness, and our ego thrives on fear. The ego owes its very existence to the illusion of being separated from the whole—little me against the rest of the world. No wonder it feels isolated, insecure, and threatened. Our true Self is securely embedded in the whole of being. What could it possibly fear? It trusts.

By saying I BELIEVE, giving both words of this phrase their full weight, we blow the sham of the ego to pieces and enter into an altogether new reality. We give expression to what it means to be fully human.

Let me express this in a somewhat whimsical image: Little X enters a little church—all perfectly harmless and uneventful. But then comes the time to recite the Creed, and Little X says, "I BE-LIEVE." Suddenly—for eyes focused on a deeper reality—roof and steeple of the church fly off, the walls crumble, time and space are suspended. All that is left is the one, all-embracing human Self in the eternal Now.

The Creed speaks in the language of the Christian religion, but also in the voice of a spirituality that lies deeper than any particular tradition. The I that says "I BELIEVE" is our true Self, the one authentic Self all humans have in common.

How do we know this is so?

"Know thyself!" reads the inscription above the entrance to Apollo's temple at Delphi, site of the famous oracle. But the ancient Greeks were not alone in this admonition of the key to wisdom. Any human being who reaches a certain stage of awareness is confronted with the challenge of self-knowledge. And as soon as we embark on the journey of self-exploration, we discover the distinction between the self we observe and a bigger Self that does the observing. We need not elaborate here on the implications. Reliable guidance to self-knowledge is readily available today, say, in the books of Eckhard Tolle or through Gempo Roshi's *Big Mind Process*. In our context here, we need only pay attention to two facts:

1. Self-observation shows us how deeply we are entangled in what we have called the ego. We can't even stop our own thoughts or the torrent of stories by which the ego keeps up the illusion of being an independent entity.
2. The more we learn to live in the now, the more we will discover the Self. As simple a practice as being alert to the opportunity each moment offers us—opportunity to breathe, to enjoy, to learn—will make us more and more at home in that Self which is one with all. There

> we experience no fear and can smile at the efforts of
> the ego to perpetuate itself.

Greek statues typically have a support leg and a free leg. Beginners in self-awareness stand with their support leg firmly in their ego consciousness. The goal of spiritual training is to shift our weight until the center of gravity rests in the true Self—our Buddha nature, as Buddhists would say; other traditions use other expressions. Saint Paul writes, "I live, yet no longer I, but Christ lives in me" (Galatians 2:20). Try to feel your way inside toward that core of yourself where you are the Watcher who is not your thoughts but can watch them. This going-inward unveils your Self to yourself—your Christself. The more we identify with this reality, the more we become uniquely ourselves and, at the same time, one with all others. Only this Self can "believe" in the full sense; only our true Self can trust unconditionally.

This is the reason that the Creed, although it is a community's declaration, does not begin with the word *we* but with *I*. This quintessential human Self—Purusha in Hindu mythology, IItoi (the Man in the Maze) in the myths of the Tohono O'Odham in Arizona, the Cosmic Christ, to give but three of many names—speaks in me and through me, because this is who I truly am.

Why make such a point of this?

If we understand the first two words of the Creed correctly, we know what "believing" means and which "I" is speaking here. This turns out to show that the Creed is not what most people think it is. Usually it is taken to be a proclamation of beliefs by which Christians distinguish themselves from all others. Rightly understood, however, it is the expression of a faith shared by all who find and acknowledge their true Self—and there is no other faith. What people call different faiths are merely different belief systems, different expressions of the one universal attitude of existential faith. Far from affirming differences between "us" and "the others," the Creed takes the sting out of these distinctions. It proclaims, in the language and imagery of the Christian tradition, a faith that is common to all human beings. Its very first word stands for that Self to which all spiritual traditions point the way.

Every one of these traditions is, as it were, a different door leading to the same sanctuary. The more we find the way to this inner sacred space and become at home there, the more freely will we be able to go in and out through the different doors. We will no longer be blocked by what seems strange to us, nor will we cling to what is familiar. Common Sense tells us how vital such an understanding is in a world still torn by wars of religion. There are still people who apparently think that one can become a better Christian at the expense of being fully human—truly humane. Anyone who puts Christian ideology above the concern for human beings could serve as an example for this incorrect understanding. Thus, what could be more urgent than to realize that the Christian profession of faith makes full humanness its cornerstone?

Since it is the quintessential human who speaks in the Creed, we will apply this insight to the text as a whole and find what each of its statements means in universal terms. Actually, if you just said I BELIEVE, and really knew what you meant by it, all that the Creed spells out would be summed up in that one phrase.

Personal reflections

Nothing is more difficult than to believe—truly to believe—in the love of another human being. Nothing is more natural than love, yet nothing is more unbelievable. That your friend loves you *goes without saying*, yet, for that very reason, *saying so* must ultimately remain unconvincing. More is needed. But what is this "more"? It is the trust—the faith—that must be supplied by the one who receives love.

My first experience of all this started as a childhood game, a staring contest with my cousin. We invented this game (or rather reinvented it, as every new generation does, I am convinced) as we lay there on a red-and-white checkered blanket on the lawn, bored and a bit resentful for still having to take an afternoon nap even though we felt so grown-up by now. It started as a contest about who could look longer into the other's eyes. Turn away and you lose. But suddenly it turned into more than a game. Maybe this began by seeing our own image mirrored small and dark in the other's pupil. What happened after that cannot easily be put into words. Somehow, we fell into each other's eyes. Like children in a fairy tale who fall into a magic pool, we were now in an enchanted land. Here one could be two and yet be one. When our eyes began to water, both of us closed them at the same time.

Later we tried to laugh it all off, but deep down we knew that we had glimpsed the real world. At that level of intense awareness, all is love. Seeing is love, breathing is love, being is love—love as a belonging that cannot be questioned or doubted.

Decades later I read the line by E. E. Cummings "i am through you so i," and I remembered. In retrospect I could recognize what the experience shared with my cousin had been: an encounter with God. Only a great poet can sum up so succinctly the insight—the conviction—that flows from an encounter like that. "i am through you so i." The you must be there for the I to find itself. Trust in you gives me trust in myself. In the encounter between the you and the I, faith is born. I am so truly I because I have faith in you. Only the I that comes about through faith can have faith.

And you? When and how have you encountered that paradox? Don't look in your memory for some big external event. For you, too, a playful moment in childhood may have provided that flash of insight never forgotten, often neglected, eminently worth recovering.

I Believe in God

❦

What does this really mean?

This initial statement contains, as in a seed, the whole of the Creed. It means that I dedicate myself in complete trust to a power greater than myself. This dedication is a commitment of my whole being— mind and body—from my heart, my innermost being, my "deep heart's core" to use an expression coined by William Butler Yeats.

Faith is far more than the sum total of beliefs. Beliefs are merely pointers; faith is profound trust in the actuality to which beliefs point. The Creed mentions beliefs, but it is a statement of faith, not of beliefs. There are many beliefs, but there is ultimately only one faith: faith in God. Beliefs are only so many windows toward the one actuality with which faith is concerned: God.

In the original Latin, the opening phrase of the Creed I BELIEVE is one word, *credo,* from which the English word *creed* derives. *Credo* is a compound of *cor* ("heart") and *do* ("I give") and means literally "I give my heart." This is an expression of faith, not of belief. The original connotation of "believing" was not so different from "giving one's heart"; the word has the same linguistic root as *love.* Today, however, the meaning has completely shifted. By belief, one gives one's intellectual assent; by faith, one gives one's heart, in total trust. And the reference point of such trust is what the word GOD signifies whenever it is properly used.

In this initial proclamation of the Creed, the word GOD is used merely as a pointer. It indicates a direction, the direction of the human heart's ultimate trust. Here GOD is not yet identified as source and goal of *my* life, *my* highest value; its meaning is still waiting to be clothed in images like the famous one by the poet Gerard Manley Hopkins: "Ground of being, and granite of it: past all grasp, God." At this point in the Creed the term GOD refers merely to the goal of an inveterate longing of the human heart for meaning. The persistence of that feeling, however, implies a deep trust that our longing can and will be stilled. This trust is the most basic faith.

How do we know this is so?

From the time we become conscious as human beings we are aware (no matter how vaguely) of the transcendent. Are you aware that everything you experience becomes in your mind a story? This starts in childhood, as soon as we become conscious. Even if you never tell this story to any person, the fact that it is a story implies a listener who takes an interest in our life story. Although we rarely focus on it, this awareness provides the contrasting background onto which we project whatever else we are aware of. In this sense we implicitly know what is meant by GOD before we know anything else: the Listener for whom we make a story out of our life.

But many people have become allergic, as it were, to the word GOD. This is understandable. Too often the G-word has been misunderstood and misused. In an attempt to point at the experiential reality without pushing the wrong linguistic button, I often use synonyms—"Ultimate Reality," "Ground of Being," "Source of Life," and the like. Yet, when we want to understand the Creed, our task is not to replace the word GOD with a different one, but rather to deepen our understanding of its meaning, especially the meaning it acquires in the context of professing one's faith.

Abraham Maslow has called attention to what he calls "peak experiences" as decisive for an understanding of religious faith. In our peak moments, we experience existential communion with an ultimate reality that transcends our own limited self. This experience is so basic that we cannot reasonably doubt its insight. It makes no sense to ask, "Is this real?" because what we encounter here is the reality that sets our standard for all that is real.

One of the leading psychiatrists of the mid-twentieth century, Maslow set himself the task of finding out what characterizes people whom one would consider models of mental health. To his great surprise he found that the psychologically healthy, highly creative, and resilient people he examined had one thing in common: mystic moments. They reported experiences in which they felt a sense of limitless belonging and experienced the goodness and beauty of all that exists—very much like the great mystics of the different spiritual traditions. Maslow spoke of "peak experiences" because his colleagues frowned upon the term "mystic," but to the end of his life he insisted that there was no difference between the two. He also found that everyone seems to have these experiences—to the extent to which one is allowed to generalize. What distinguishes truly great human beings from ordinary people is that they let their lives be shaped by their mystic insights. For instance, they behave toward others as one behaves toward people to whom one belongs; they live gratefully aware of the goodness and beauty we encounter everywhere.

You may remember moments in which you were most truly yourself precisely because you lost yourself, say, looking at the starry sky or at a sleeping baby. Suddenly the sharp border by which you set yourself off from others fades away. In those peak moments we can get a taste of what the mystics call communion with God, though all the emphasis is on limitless belonging, not on any notion of that *to which* we belong. It would seem impossible to experience this deep belonging and not to commit oneself wholeheartedly, for it fulfills our deepest desire. But for most of us the memory of our peak experience fades. What persists is mostly a vague longing to belong. At the outset of our spiritual life, GOD is merely a direction in which our deepest longing points.

Why make such a point of this?

Nothing is more important to us humans than to find meaning in life. We are able to bear great hardship, great pain, as long as we perceive the difficulties we are undergoing to be meaningful. If, on the other hand, we lose the sense of meaning, even the most pleasant surroundings and the kindest company will not save us from despair.

Ask yourself: What gives my life meaning? Whatever answer you give, it will boil down to some notion of belonging. Thus your own experience proves to you that only a sense of belonging makes human life meaningful. We need to remember this insight: Meaning springs from belonging.

A second crucial insight is this: Our deepest belonging is our belonging to God. But wait! Do not assume that we start out by knowing what we mean by God, and then affirm our belonging. Rather, we must turn this around and ask: Where is my deepest belonging anchored? Where is it anchored beyond the realm of all perishable phenomena that come and go? The answer to this question will show to each one of us what we personally mean by "God" (when this term is correctly used). The particular form in which we express our faith in God is not of ultimate importance; it can change. What does matter most is this: to discover the ocean depth in which we have sunk our anchor of meaning, to recognize that this is what "God" means for us, and to let this meaning flow into our daily living.

Is it important to actually say, "I believe in God," or "I have faith in God"? The answer is yes. To put this into so many words—even if I say them only to myself in silence—can be a decisive step in my spiritual life, for every time I remember my belonging I drink from the Source of Meaning. This gives dedication to my life; it helps me avoid dead-end roads of alienation, and keeps me from feeling orphaned in the universe. It helps me go forward with a clear awareness of what ultimately matters. Expressing faith in God gives a firm foundation to joyful, grateful, and creative living.

This foundation is made all the greater when I join with others in proclaiming our basic faith in God, a faith that unites all human beings. I grow stronger in my consciousness of a worldwide communion. After all, we share with all other humans on this planet the potential to become aware of our deepest belonging and to find in it the Source of Meaning—whether or not we speak of "God." This is also the basis for our mutual belonging to one another. Nothing is more urgently needed today than this sense of mutual belonging among all human beings—which then expands to include the nonhuman universe as well.

There are many religions, many beliefs, but only one faith. We can (and must) learn to take our faith more seriously than the beliefs in which that faith has found expression up till now. The present calls for a different expression, if faith is to have a future. Religious beliefs always run the risk of dividing us; they have power to do so. But faith has even greater power to unite us.

The Apostles' Creed is the Christian profession of faith at Baptism. Immersion in the baptismal waters is a sacramental sign for birth into a new life: God's life in us; our life in God—the triune God. The formula I—BELIEVE—IN GOD points from the very start toward a Trinitarian understanding. "God" stands for the unfathomable Mystery out of which I come and to which I am related. The "I" stands for the human Self, in whom the universe becomes explicitly conscious of God and of itself. And to "believe" stands for the third dimension of that divine life which unites the two poles of God and "I" in the dynamic creative process of living and loving. Step by step the Creed will reveal what this first, all-important sentence anticipates.

Personal reflections

The words of a small boy whom his mother tucks in at bedtime still ring in my memory. He is afraid of the dark, and his mother assures him, "No need to be afraid; God is always near you." "Yes," he answers, "I know, but I want a God with skin on." Don't we all? We have been deprived of seeing God's body all around us, when society programmed us to conceive of God as separated from the world and as "pure Spirit." We hardly noticed that by making God "immaterial" in the sense of having no material body or form, God became "immaterial" also, in the sense of lacking tangible relevance and importance. For Mary Oliver, a poet who never lost the child's vision of "a God with skin on,"

> *it is not hard to understand*
> *where God's body is,*
> *everywhere and everything; shore and the vast*
> *fields of water, the accidental and the intended*
> *over here and over there. . . .*

She finds it everywhere and in everything. This should not come as a surprise to any Christian who takes the Incarnation seriously. The incessant and inexorable divine Self–outpouring by which "the Word was made flesh" will burst any dike with which a theologian might try to hold its rushing flood in bounds. The priest at the Eucharist who in Christ's name says "this is my Body" cannot limit the meaning of these words to the bread he holds in his hands. Your body, as Saint Paul tells us, is a temple of the Holy Spirit, but where does your body end? Is it interwoven with the whole universe? And if so, is not the whole universe your body— Christ's body, temple of the Holy Spirit, body of God?

It is so dense and apparent—that body of God, says Mary Oliver—*and all the same I am still unsatisfied. . . . Where, do you suppose, is His pale and wonderful mind?* "Show us the Father," says Philip in John's Gospel, and Jesus replies, "Whoever sees Me, sees the Father." Christian tradition calls the manifestation of God in all that exists "the Cosmic Christ." The whole universe is God's body. But if we are in this way surrounded by God's manifestation, from where springs our longing for God un-manifest? Could this longing itself be a divine urge in the depth of our being?

Did you ever receive an anonymous gift? Do you remember how this made you feel? My own recollection is that anonymous gifts make me feel at a loss. Much as I may appreciate the gift, it is above all my relationship to the giver that matters to me. Relationship is the most important aspect of gift-giving and receiving. All the *dense and apparent* manifestation of God is a gift. So, what stirs within us is the urge to give thanks for that gift, and we turn toward the Giver, the un-manifest God, the pure Love that pours itself out *as* the manifest.

We can only speak in metaphors. Each metaphor has its strengths and its limitations. One reason I am fond of seeing the universe as God's body is that this metaphor could immensely increase our reverence for Mother Earth (and thus give our male God image a healthy jolt). Can you imagine what it might do to our imagination if we could get ourselves to recognize the injuries we have inflicted on our environment as wounds in God's body? Are there aspects of your upbringing that favor or block that notion? How does the idea that the universe is God's body strike you personally?

The Father

—

What does this really mean?

By introducing the name FATHER for God, the Creed is beginning
to express the universal human faith in specifically Christian terms.
It remains, however, the same faith. It is in light of this basic human
faith in God that its specific Christian formulation will have to be
interpreted and understood. There can be different beliefs through
which faith is expressed, there can be different stages of faith development, but faith as such is a courageous trust in "a Power
greater than ourselves." The term FATHER makes explicit that we
trust in God as loving. Implicitly, faith always presupposes this conviction, for we can ultimately only trust in love.

Jesus' favorite way of expressing his faith was by calling God
"Abba," a term of endearment that expresses a child's trust in a father's love. To many Christians the image of God as FATHER has become so familiar that they tend to forget that it is an image. Many
others today find that the exclusive use of the father-image for God
can cause far-reaching psychological and sociological distortions.
Too many masculine aspects get unconsciously projected onto one's
God-view; too many motherly ones get overlooked and lost. This
bolsters male chauvinism in society, and can easily lead to imagin-
ing God like one's own father—with all the tensions this can produce. Faith in God resembles a child's trust in a mother at least as
closely as in a father. No matter how meaningful or time-honored
a given image, it will fall short of expressing some aspect for which
other images are better suited. We will do well to remember this

and stay flexible, above all when we deal with that which calls us into a trust beyond our imagination.

If we still call God FATHER, we do so because Jesus did. If we keep this in mind, the use of FATHER in the Creed identifies one lineage of faith—that of Jesus—but who could want to restrict all faith to that lineage? The tree of human faith is ancient and has many older branches. Faith did not come into existence with its expression in particular Christian beliefs. But from this point on, the Creed unfolds now the Christian expression of faith. Those who prefer a different expression of universal faith may still find this one enriching. The more we come alive to the essence of faith, the more we appreciate and enjoy the great variety of its expressions.

The God-space (analogous to cosmic space) that our hearts have been exploring since the inception of human life is so vast that explorers can bring back apparently contradictory reports that, nevertheless, agree. In God all opposites coincide, as Nicholas of Cusa (1401–1464) realized. The explorations of Jewish, Christian, and Muslim mystics stress the personal aspect of ultimate belonging. Primal traditions—Native American, for instance—and some branches of Hinduism use images of Father, Mother, or Ancestor for God. Calling God FATHER implies that we can experience the ultimate Source of all as personally and caringly related to us. And yet, faith in God as personal does not imply the mistaken notion that God is "a person." Nothing justifies us in limiting God by our concept of person. Yet to speak of God in personal terms is justified by our experience of a personal relationship to God.

How do we know this is so?

In the best, most alive moments of life, when we are most truly and fully ourselves—in our peak moments—we experience what has been described as "limitless belonging." When we explore our sense of belonging, we discover that belonging is always mutual. Mutuality becomes more and more intense the more personal the bond becomes. There is even a kind of mutuality between us and things that belong to us. Our belongings make certain demands on us—care, thoughtfulness, patience. From there we can progress to plants, animals, and humans, and we find that from level to level the personal aspect of the relationship increases and mutuality deepens. This progression ultimately points in the direction we call "God." In the first verse of Psalm 63, "God, you are *my* God," the possessive pronoun *my* is more appropriate and carries greater meaning than in any other context. Only God can be fully and inseparably *mine*, because only to God do I fully and inseparably belong. Before we know anything else about God, we know God as the direction of our longing and belonging. In our relationship to the Source of Being, mutuality reaches its unsurpassable climax.

Since I am a person and this bond of belonging is deeply personal, I express my relationship to Ultimate Reality in personal terms and in images like FATHER. In doing so, I am ascribing to God all the perfections of personhood and none of its faults. After all, how could I be a person if Ultimate Reality were impersonal?

One of my Zen teachers, Eido Shimano Roshi, often spoke of our fleeting human existence as a wave that rises from the ocean and sinks back into it. This image seemed to me to miss something essential. So I asked, "As a wave I have personal consciousness and freedom; am I to lose all this when I flow back into the ocean?" Eido Roshi's answer: "From where could the wave have personal consciousness and freedom if the ocean did not have it?" This means that all the positive values we associate with personhood—our own and that of others—are a gift and manifestation of the Un-manifest. The wave has nothing that the ocean does not have. So it makes sense for me as a person to relate to that aspect of the Un-manifest in personal terms. Jesus did so by using the term FATHER.

Why make such a point of this?

By cultivating a personal relationship with Ultimate Reality, we can greatly increase our joy in life. This relationship makes gratefulness possible, and gratefulness is the key to joy. What we take for granted does not give us joy, but whatever we are grateful for does. Thus, joy is the happiness that does not depend on what happens. We hold the key to joy in our own hands: gratefulness. And just as gratefulness is most intense when it is personal, so is the joy it triggers. Awareness of being personally related to the divine Ground of Being is the basis for ultimate gratefulness and thus for the deepest joy. By calling God FATHER we express a personal relationship that makes gratitude and joy possible.

Calling God FATHER distinguishes the Jesus tradition of faith from all others—yet at the same time it relates this Christian tradition more deeply to all others. Because Christians call God FATHER, they must recognize all other humans—in fact, all other creatures—as their sisters and brothers, and treat them accordingly. This makes the whole Earth God's household and each living being a full and cherished member—an image that could certainly increase our sense of belonging to this planet and of being responsible for it.

Personal reflections

On Fathers' Day, when our pastor invites the fathers in the congregation to rise for a special blessing, it is with full conviction that I, too, stand up. The anguish I have suffered for my many spiritual sons and daughters (and also the joy) can certainly compare with those of the father of twelve children I once dreamed of becoming. To have a child is all too easy for a man. Too often we hear of unprepared men leaving their families to fend for themselves, or remaining in the home but neglecting their duty to love, with suffering the result for the mother and children. And, as we all know, true fathering is quite a different matter, a task that demands all the best qualities of character and, above all, patient love. "God is like the father you wish you'd had," said a boy in a juvenile prison. When the Creed calls God FATHER, it is not as the Source and

Originator of all there is, but as a loving, caring Presence in our lives. Unless we can give to the metaphor of God as FATHER the heartwarming ring that Jesus gave it, we might do better not to use it at all.

Lucky are those who carry with them memories of loving parents. Do you? Luckier still, those whose children will carry such memories in their hearts. It will make all the difference for their— the parents' no less than the childrens'—understanding of God's relationship to us.

What I have in mind here are, above all, heartwarming memories. They need not be especially noble, lofty, or momentous. What most affects us are memories of love in all its quirky humor. Yes, humor, one of the most outstanding qualities of God's love. A humor that (in keeping with its linguistic context) never humiliates us, but makes us humble and humane if we allow it to sink in.

In his poem "My Papa's Waltz," Theodore Roethke has captured a tart sweetness I can readily associate with God's love, in spite of whiskey on the father's breath. Mother Church may frown, but "the Father will dance" (as in the delightful song by Cary Landry and Carol Jean Kinghorn), and we could do worse than cling to God's shirt.

> *The whiskey on your breath*
> *Could make a small boy dizzy;*
> *But I hung on like death:*
> *Such waltzing was not easy.*
>
> *We romped until the pans*
> *Slid from the kitchen shelf;*
> *My mother's countenance*
> *Could not unfrown itself.*
>
> *The hand that held my wrist*
> *Was battered on one knuckle;*

Deeper Than Words

At every step you missed
My right ear scraped a buckle.

You beat time on my head
With a palm caked hard by dirt,
Then waltzed me off to bed
Still clinging to your shirt.

The Father Almighty

~

What does this really mean?

Having proclaimed our faith in God, whom Jesus taught us to recognize as a caring Father, we now call this fatherly God ALMIGHTY. This sequence is revealing. We do not speak of an omnipotent God, but first call God Father and then proclaim our faith that God—*as* Father—is ALMIGHTY. This shows that we do not start out with some philosophical notion of omnipotence.

The very meaning of ALMIGHTY in the Creed is defined by its position: only in the context of God's fatherly love do we call God Almighty. Nothing is omnipotent except love. Life experience teaches us that only love has the power to put even the messiest situations in order by giving them a new meaning. Saint Augustine's enigmatic sentence *Ordo est amoris* may be understood to mean that almighty love ultimately does bring order to our seemingly chaotic world. Faith in God as father is faith in ALMIGHTY love.

How do we know this is so?

All evidence seems to contradict the very possibility that God could be both loving and ALMIGHTY. Given the violence, destruction, and suffering we see all around us, God's love seems ineffectual and far from omnipotent. Or, worse, if God is indeed omnipotent but allows all this to happen, God is monstrous. This dilemma cannot be resolved from an "objective" conceptual perspective of detached speculation.

Consult your personal experience. For what do you long most

deeply: a painless existence or a meaningful one? Would not the greatest pain be the lack of meaning in life? Humans can survive under conditions of unimaginable deprivation, yet when life loses its meaning they cannot survive. But what makes life meaningful? The answer is *love*. I ask you, is it not love that gives meaning to *your* life? But love must be freely given; it cannot be forced or bought. Love presupposes freedom. Here we touch upon the crucial point. Our human dignity hinges on the right use of freedom. The converse is the abuse of freedom, which causes suffering for ourselves and others. Fearing that, should we then want freedom to be eliminated so as to get rid of suffering? No freedom, no love; no love, no meaning; no meaning, the worst possible suffering: meaninglessness. The only way off this dead-end road lies in the opposite direction: love can give meaning even to suffering—and so overcome it.

There is a life-denying way of suffering: "against the grain," as it were, resentfully. And there is a life-affirming way: "with the grain," lovingly. But what shall we tell those who find themselves incapable of giving meaning to their suffering through love? It is not a matter of *telling* them anything, for this would prove our lack of reverence for their suffering. We can only silently stand with them. Keep in mind that when a child suffers, the parent suffers even more. A single tear shed by a child shatters the philosophical construct of an omnipotent God who cannot suffer.

By calling God first FATHER and only then ALMIGHTY, the Creed implies that wherever there is suffering, it is God as loving Father who suffers. This does not take away the pain, but gives meaning to it through love.

Why make such a point of this?

By calling God FATHER, we begin to regard ourselves and God's whole cosmic household in a new light, the light of love. By calling God's fatherly love ALMIGHTY, we imply that its light shines not only *into* the darkness, as light always does. The light of love shines "*in* the darkness" (John 1:5), in suffering, in confusion, in all that we will never understand. Love makes darkness itself shine. This opens altogether new possibilities for dealing creatively with the shadow side of reality. Words can only serve as pointers; we must put this to the test in our own dark hours. Those who have done so, those who have suffered lovingly, have discovered the transformative power of love.

Personal reflections

"Is God really everywhere?" a child asks the Sunday-school teacher. "Yes!" is the answer, "God is present everywhere." "In our attic, too?" "Why, of course." "And in our basement, too?" "Yes, yes, my dear. God is present even in your basement." "Gotcha! We don't *have* a basement!" You can play such mental games with God's omnipotence just as well as with God's omnipresence. Can God make a square circle? Obviously not. This, however, does not prove that God's power is limited, but rather that the question is stupid.

The word ALMIGHTY tends to lure us into misunderstandings. It conjures up images of some super-king who makes everyone and everything obey his will (yes, "his," for this is certainly a male fantasy). We forget that God "stepped back," as Jewish tradition puts it, to let the universe and every creature within it do its thing. God gives all beings freedom to be themselves. God looks at them with a mother's eyes, and says, "Yes, you can do it!" much as Cesar Chavez empowered the downtrodden with the same words (they sound still more encouraging in Spanish), *"Si, se puedes!"* All of God's power flows into empowering us with that motherly "Yes." When I come to the word ALMIGHTY in the Creed, I read it as "Yes." God's almightiness is the power of ultimate affirmation.

In his well-known prayer, "i thank you God for most this amazing day," the poet E. E. Cummings thanks God "for everything which is natural which is infinite which is yes." He speaks of us human beings as "lifted from the no of all nothing" by God's "yes." But God not only lifts the universe out of "the no of all nothing,"

God *speaks* the encouraging "yes" that lets all things unfold and be themselves. We could even say that God simply *is* Yes.

For another poet, Jessica Powers, "yes is the one need of my whole life," and

> *. . . I would guess*
> *heaven for me   will be an infinite*
> *flowering of one species   a measureless sheer*
> *beatitude of yes*

Cummings went so far as to say, "i imagine that yes is the only living thing." And he counsels us, "forgetting if, remember yes."

Have you ever experienced a moment when "out of the lie of no, rises a truth of yes"? If so, you know from experience what we mean when, in the Creed, we call God ALMIGHTY. We can usually see this only in retrospect. Looking back on a juncture in our life when all the circumstances shouted "NO!" to all we hoped for, we see now, years later, that somehow a *yes* emerged after all. This loving *yes* created new and unforeseen beginnings that surpassed all our hopes. In the context of our profession of faith, this recognition means even more. It implies our commitment to empower others, our commitment to let the wind of God's almighty power swell our sails, so that through all we do and suffer, the truth of *yes* will rise out of the lie of *no*. For this we may pray with another cummings poem:

> *may i be gay*
> *like every lark who lifts his life from all the dark*
> *who wings his why*
> *beyond because and sings an if*
> *of day to yes*

Creator of Heaven and Earth

※

What does this really mean?

By calling God CREATOR, Christians express their trust that all things and events must be ultimately meaningful because they flow from that deepest wellspring of meaning that we call God. The notion of divine creativity evokes associations of wise planning, of thorough and detailed designing, of caring maintenance. The driving force of all creativity is love. Whatever there is, is a gift freely given, and this makes all of it meaningful.

We have to take great care, however, to avoid the mistaken idea that creation implies some external impetus, some kickoff by the CREATOR. Divine creativity works from within. It is one with the impulse of every creature to become itself. Goethe's Doctor Faustus wanted to know what "holds the world together at its innermost core." The creative principle he was looking for was love. Love—in the sense of an active *yes* to belonging—moves even the smallest particle of the universe from within.

HEAVEN AND EARTH means everything there is—"all that is visible and all that is invisible" says another Christian creed, but that, too, remains metaphor. Through the influence of Eastern thought, many people in the West today are familiar with the distinction between manifest and un-manifest. This pair of concepts may parallel what HEAVEN AND EARTH meant to those who formulated the Creed. Thus, we may take EARTH to mean all that is manifest in outer and inner reality, and HEAVEN as all that is "hidden in God" (Colossians 3:3)—in the pregnant womb of divine Nothing and

Emptiness. The great theologian Ramon Panikkar says poignantly, "The Nothing out of which God creates everything is God."

We must continue to search for helpful images and metaphors, but never forget, they are no more than that. HEAVEN in this clause of the Creed does not refer to a place of eternal bliss, but rather to the fountainhead of God's creative action, which is the word's original meaning in the Hebrew Bible.

How do we know this is so?

When we look around us, we spontaneously experience nature as meaningful. Things tell us something, though not in words. We encounter in them a greater Presence that they embody, as it were. Sometimes this fills us with awe—in a thunderstorm, maybe, or when we stand on the rim of the Grand Canyon. Everything natural speaks to us, though not in concepts—or rather every Presence speaks to us through all we can perceive. This experience stands behind the biblical notion that "God spoke . . . and it was." This is poetic language inspired by the experience that my listening heart can hear God speaking to me through all of creation. And this experience is accessible to anyone whose faith is attuned enough to overcome fear-based self-deception. We experience a trustworthiness of reality that is expressed, for instance, in the "laws of nature." So it makes sense when H. R. Niebuhr says, "There is faithfulness at the heart of all things." The human heart spontaneously senses the heartbeat of a Presence whose faithfulness calls forth our faith.

We can also use a slightly different approach. We recognize all there is (including our own mind and body) as a "given reality"—in other words, as a gift. From there, our mind traces everything back to an ultimate Source, and conceives the idea of God as CREATOR. From the outside this looks like a case of anthropomorphic personification; but from the inside it can be experienced as the genuine discovery of a "Giver of all Gifts" who meets us in every given moment. Our own creativity consists of what we make out of the opportunity given to us at each moment. In this way we participate in the ongoing process of creation. From the point of view of the little ego this has been seen as "co-creation." In our most creative moments, however, our true Self can experience a still closer union than the "co-" suggests. The very energy of the CREATOR is flowing through us. "You are here to enable the divine purpose of the universe to unfold," says Eckhard Tolle. "That is how important you are!"

Why make such a point of this?

It greatly improves our attitude toward the world around us, if we see it not as an environment simply happening as the result of blind mechanical forces, but look deeper and discover at its core a faithfulness prepared with love and care as our home. A home is something one has to take care of, something for which one is responsible.

As long as we remember the CREATOR is an image, it may be understood as referring to the arising of form out of emptiness, with a much-needed emphasis on wisdom and compassion as the driving force. Then the reality to which this image points will not only fill us with awe, but will inspire our sense of accountability. In the midst of our ecological crisis it helps to be reminded that we are responsible for nature (including our own bodies) as God's creative Self-expression. To see HEAVEN AND EARTH—the inner and the outer, mind and matter—equally devised by creative love, makes for a balanced worldview and for conscientious action.

An ancient layer of human religiosity uses the image of the CREATOR, and this image is still vividly alive for people in many parts of the world. With their faith we can establish a conscious link every time we refer in the Creed to God as CREATOR OF HEAVEN AND EARTH. Our survival, no less than that of the Guarani people, living in the endangered Amazon rain forest, depends on a conscious and active affirmation of the bonds uniting us with all humans on Earth. Faith, no matter how differently expressed, is one of the strongest of these bonds.

The biblical creation story speaks of God as creating the world "in the beginning." We must, however, beware of the mistaken notion of some initial impulse, given by a divine influence from the outside. Creative Love is at work at the innermost core of the smallest particle of the universe—and not only at some starting point, but always. When we keep this in mind, faith in creation will make us creative.

Personal reflections

Irises are not just flowers to me; they are friends. They are sisters to me from way back in my father's garden, when I had to stretch and stand on tiptoe to smell them, for they were taller than me. Their watery fragrance floats through my childhood memories. Later I learned to associate this teasing, tentative perfume with the girls who were my earliest childhood crushes. The iris awakened me to beauty then, and still does today.

In seven decades the lure of these fanciful blossoms has not diminished for me, and the golden fuzz on their bearded, drooping sepals with their fingerprint-like veins invites not only the bee but my own glance deep into the sunlit wedding tent of the translucent petals. I look and look and lose myself in this looking. Time stands still when I stand before an iris. Time is no more. All is now. And in this now, the iris comes forth from "the no of all nothing" as an ever-so-delicate, ever-so-real "Yes!" All of Van Gogh's irises are summed up and surpassed in this single one, moving ever so slightly in the morning breeze.

When this happens, I have long left my thoughts far behind. They cannot keep up with my awareness. It has plummeted down to the point where this iris springs forth: now and now and now it leaps from nonbeing into being—together with the firethorn bush behind it, with the rail fence, with the sky and its towering cloud, together with myself. With every breath I can say, "I am." With every heartbeat I can affirm being out of nonbeing. Suddenly I understand what John Cage wrote:

Each something is a celebration of the nothing that supports it.

Does this find an echo in your heart before you start to figure out what precisely it means? I personally put my faith in the process of continuous creation that this line implies. I trust that process; I entrust myself to it. It is not an impersonal process, but the deepest of all personal relationships. Can you make a connection between the Nothing that supports everything—the Un-manifest that manifests itself in all there is—and that mysterious Presence whom Jesus calls *Abba*, Father?

And in Jesus Christ

What does this really mean?

The correct understanding of this phrase hinges on the little word AND. Does this AND add anything? We have already proclaimed our faith in God; what could be added to God? Faith is total commitment; nothing can be added to what is total. So, this AND does not imply addition but clarification, as when we say "the sun and its warmth will do you good."

In saying that we believe in God AND IN JESUS CHRIST, we take one further step in making explicit how we experience God: as Father, as almighty Love, as Creator, and now as the One whom we encounter in Jesus Christ. One of the earliest Christian sayings runs like this: "Have you seen your Sister, your Brother? You have your God." According to biblical understanding, every human being bears God's image. We must admit that the likeness of that image is often blurred or even defaced. Those who met Jesus, however, were amazed at how easy it was to feel face to face with God when he looked at them—how easy it was to hear God's voice, as it were, when he talked with them. In the Gospels they bore witness to this amazing fact. And ever since, Christians are those who have encountered God in and through JESUS CHRIST.

Note that no exclusivity is implied here. We can encounter God in Jesus Christ, but why should this be the only way to encounter God? When we say that the sun and its warmth does us good, are we excluding its light? We can encounter God in innumerable ways. For Christians, Jesus Christ is the focal point of all their encounters with the divine.

Let us not forget, Christians believe not merely in Jesus, nor merely in Christ, but IN JESUS CHRIST. This appellation connects two poles: Jesus, a historic person distinct from us, and Christ, the human/divine unity identical with our true Self. I must hold these two poles together in creative tension. There is always the danger of letting their connection snap. Then Jesus no longer provides an objective reference point for the Christ reality within me and, deprived of this guiding standard, it can be distorted at will by my self-deception. Both poles need constant attention. I must learn to understand, better and better, what my commitment to the way of Jesus means, and I must live ever more consciously from my own true Self, which is the Christ within me. Dynamic faith IN JESUS CHRIST demands that I rise to this double task.

How do we know this is so?

Our knowledge of Jesus is mediated through others. The Christ in us we know firsthand, even if we have never heard of Jesus.

We turn first to this Christ experience. "Love makes blind," an old saying goes. But it is equally true that lovers look deeply into each other's eyes and hearts—so deeply at times they catch a glimpse of the divine in the other. In this experience lies the seed for understanding the true Self as the divine Self. The Bible expresses this by referring to humans as created "in God's image and likeness." That likeness will shine forth all the more splendidly as we come to realize our true identity—the Christ in us. In this sense, one doesn't have to be a Christian to know Christ. You know Christ when you know your Self.

How do we find that Self? To find it is the goal of every spiritual practice, and the method is always the same: learning to live in the present moment. Different traditions have developed many different ways to facilitate this learning process. One example is grateful living. You can be grateful *for* the past, but you can only be grateful in the present. You can be grateful that you have a future, but you are grateful *now*. And whenever you are present now, your awareness has switched the Self. As people come to know their authentic Self, they become acquainted with the inner reality that Christians call Christ.

How we can know Jesus, and especially what connection we can make between Jesus and Christ, will depend on our upbringing, on the circumstances of our life, on our cultural conditioning, and so on. A Christian child might grow up with a continuous confusion between Jesus and God. A Jewish child might discover that even mentioning Jesus is asking for trouble. If we are lucky, we might meet Christians who are true followers of Jesus and bring the joy of God's love to everyone they meet. But we may have the misfortune to meet people who claim a special closeness to Jesus and are obnoxious. The culture of our ancestors may have been destroyed in the name of Jesus by well-intentioned but misguided missionaries. Or we may have grown up in a culture in which the most admirable traits are somehow connected with Jesus, from Handel's *Messiah* to 12-step programs. A fair-minded approach to Jesus demands a colossal effort for many people to overcome either negative prejudice or biased exclusiveness. A book like *Meeting Jesus Again for the First Time*, by Marcus Borg, has been an eye-opener for many people. In any event, we owe it to ourselves to get as clear a picture as we can of Jesus, whose impact on history set in motion a nonviolent social revolution that is still in full swing: the struggle to overcome the love of power by the power of love.

Mere theoretical knowledge will not suffice to comprehend what this clause of the Creed really means. Three elements must come together before we can experientially know what it means to believe in God AND IN JESUS CHRIST:

1. We must have at least a budding awareness of our deepest Self, the Christ within us.
2. We must acquire at least a rudimentary knowledge of Jesus in history and of the nonviolent social revolution for which he gave his life.

3. We must set our heart on realizing our divine Self (the Christ in us) by joining the great human cause for which Jesus lived and died.

Why make such a point of this?

Faith IN JESUS (as) CHRIST implies we recognize in Jesus our own human/divine self—the Self that bears God's image and is alive with God's own Life-breath, to use the poetic language with which the Bible speaks about Adam, the human prototype. This is not a belief in something outside ourselves, but existential trust that God's loving presence can be realized in us and, through us, in the world. Proclaiming our faith in this presence is already the first step toward a new world order.

This helps us understand why faith IN JESUS CHRIST creates no separation between Christians and others, as was often assumed in the past. On the contrary, the important message of this phrase in the Creed is we can encounter God in a human being—in any human being, even in ourselves. The divine wants to manifest itself in the human, if only we open our hearts to this possibility. It takes all of us to rise to this challenge. Christians cannot do it by themselves; it is a task for the human family as a whole, its most important task.

The decisive AND in this phrase ties together faith in the divine as all-transcending with faith in the divine as immanent in the world—and in an exemplary manner IN JESUS CHRIST. This gives our faith in God a solid point of reference—"The point of intersection of the timeless with time" as T. S. Eliot called it—of the Christ in each of us with Jesus in history. It also gives to faith a clear direction for action: toward "the Kingdom of God"—a world order based on love—through nonviolent revolution.

Personal reflections

It was in the rolling hills near Bologna, in the charming Emilia Romagna region of Italy, and I was privileged to be part of a meeting held in the historic Palazzo Loup. For three days, some six or eight of us sat around a large table, excitedly discussing questions of science and spirituality. Nicholas Humphrey, the British psychologist, sat next to me, and we soon discovered we had more in common than adjoining places at the conference table. We went for a long hike together, and Nick generously gave me a copy of *Seeing Red: A Study in Consciousness*—the only copy he had with him of his latest book, just published.

Humphrey starts his investigation by asking what happens when we see something red. This "feeling of redness" tells us something about our environment. But are the sensations something that happens to us? No, says Humphrey, they are something we do; they are our reactions to an environmental stimulus and can be traced back in an unbroken evolutionary line of descent to the way single cells respond to stimulation. Their semipermeable membrane lets certain substances in and rejects others. Thus they define themselves, as it were, by their likes and dislikes. More highly developed animals will do so more obviously, as when a cat hunts for mice and hides from dogs. And think how distinct our human likes and dislikes are, how they distinguish us from one another. We define ourselves by what we value and what we reject. Our preferences and our aversions contribute much to our sense of self.

Nick Humphrey's study in consciousness is full of thought-provoking insights, but I am focusing here on the author's notion of self, which leads him to climax his book with a poem in which Gerard Manley Hopkins coins the verb "to selve." A thing "selves" by saying, through its very being, what it is. Thus, a bird—a kingfisher, in Hopkins's poem—a dragonfly, a bell, or anything else may cry out, as it were, "What I do is me: for that I came." This sentence from Hopkins's poem is the last line of *Seeing Red*. "But this sonnet has six more lines. Why did you not quote those?" I asked. "I just don't like them," was Nick Humphrey's answer. This made me go back and study the poem carefully.

> As kingfishers catch fire, dragonflies draw flame;
> As tumbled over rim in roundy wells
> Stones ring; like each tucked string tells, each hung bell's
> Bow swung finds tongue to fling out broad its name;
> Each mortal thing does one thing and the same:
> Deals out that being indoors each one dwells;
> Selves—goes itself; myself it speaks and spells,
> Crying What I do is me: for that I came.
>
> I say more: the just man justices;
> Keeps grace: that keeps all his goings graces;
> Acts in God's eye what in God's eye he is—
> Christ—for Christ plays in ten thousand places,
> Lovely in limbs, and lovely in eyes not his
> To the Father through the features of men's faces.

The poet refers back to the first eight lines of his sonnet (the octet) and anticipates the last six lines (the sextet) with the exclamation: "I say more." And what is this "more"? Its essence is the switch of focus from "selving" to "justicing," another word the poet had to coin to fill his need.

"Each mortal thing does one thing and the same," namely, it "selves." But the "more" consists of this: "The just man justices." Sam Keen, a longtime friend and a neighbor to my hermitage, shared with me his vision of what religion will have to look like in the future. Sam is deeply committed to social justice. So it came as no surprise when I read in his manuscript, "For better and worse we are members one of another—a community of justice-in-the-making." This sounded to me like a comment on Hopkins. Selving produces distinct individuals, but justicing produces communities in harmony. The poet triggers an association with harmony when he describes justicing as "keeping grace." As if hitting two notes at once, the phrase suggests both a dancer's keeping pace with the rhythm and the grace of her movement. By doing so, the dancer "acts in God's eye what in God's eye he is—Christ." By being in step with a cosmic rhythm, in tune with a cosmic harmony, a creature will "say more" than "this is me." Yes, it is "me," yet not in separation, but one with every "me" and so infinitely more. The "me" is now a member of the Cosmic Christ.

Till late in the night, I sat jotting down for Nick Humphrey my comments on the lines of the poem that he had omitted. No matter how far back you go—to the "likes or dislikes" of a cell, or even the compatibility or incompatibility of molecules or atoms—all this is already of one piece with what in humans becomes the conscious-ness of the Cosmic Christ. It would make no sense for Hopkins to say "Jesus" where he uses "Christ." Yet, in Jesus, as potentially in every one of us, justicing adjusts the me-consciousness to the Christ-consciousness.

Can you somehow connect "justicing" with your personal experi-ence and consciousness? Have you noticed that justice within you (an adjustment to what is right) makes you work for justice in the world around you? I do not mean judgmental activism, but inner harmony creating outer harmony, be it in the way you furnish your room or in the political action you engage in. The latter became so central for Jesus' justicing that he paid for it with his life. He truly was the just man who justices—and so, Christ.

God's Only Son

～

What does this really mean?

"Son of God" as well as ONLY SON are expressions that have come into the Creed from the Hebrew Bible. They must therefore be understood in the sense they had in their original Jewish context, not in a Hellenistic sense. Jesus is not proclaimed to be the son of a god as, for instance, Castor and Pollux were sons of Zeus in Greek mythology. Not unlike the English expression "son of a gun," the Hebrew idiom "Son of God" refers to likeness, not to descent. The biblical prototype of a son of God is Adam (the "earthling," the human par excellence) created like every human being, "in God's image" and destined to show forth "God's likeness." Jesus is called "Son of God" and "the second Adam" for having fulfilled that destiny to such a degree that others saw in him what God is like.

The expression ONLY SON must equally be understood against the background of the Hebrew Bible. There it may mean a son who has no brothers, but it may also be used to stress the great love of the parent for a son who does have brothers. In Genesis, chapter 22, for instance, Isaac is called Abraham's "only son" although his brother also figures in the story. "Uniquely beloved" would be a more accurate English rendering and less misleading. ONLY SON, in the sense of "uniquely beloved," carries no exclusive connotations; each child of a parent is "uniquely beloved," no matter how many there are. Jesus' divine sonship is not exclusive but includes every single human being. All who trust, implicitly at least, in love and compassion as the ultimate good, are—in and with Jesus the son of God—sons and daughters of God who is Love. "To as

many as received him he gave authority to become children of God"
(John 1:12).

Is the relationship between God and Jesus Christ not unique?
Of course it is. But so is yours. The relationship between God and
every human being is unique and irreplaceable—in ever-new variations of the Christ theme. "For Christ plays in ten thousand places,
lovely in limbs, and lovely in eyes not his to the Father" through the
features of our human faces (G. M. Hopkins). The First Letter of
John calls out with amazement, "Behold what love the Father has
shown us, that we should be called children of God—and such we
are" (I John 3:1).

How do we know this is so?

The linguistic background of biblical idioms like "Son of God" and
ONLY SON is accessible to interested readers; one needs no scholarly background. Any decent public library will have biblical dic-
tionaries, concordances, and commentaries. Just as professionals
need to keep abreast of current research in their field, continued
study is necessary for those who are conscientious about matters of
faith. Not to remain on a Sunday-school level of understanding is
a mature person's responsibility.

Still more important than book knowledge, however, is personal
experience: "No one knows the Father but the Son," we read in the
Gospel (Matthew 11:2). And this is good news indeed, for it means
all who do know a caring Higher Power are sons and daughters of
God. Such knowledge can only come from experience, but it is
accessible to everyone of us. Millions of people in 12-step programs
know this, and so do countless others who reached a point where
nothing would help them anymore but reliance on a power greater
than ourselves. Once we come to experience that power for which
a father's caring love is a fitting image, we understand that Jesus
can be called GOD'S ONLY SON, for we experience ourselves as
uniquely beloved sons and daughters of God—*as we understand*
God.

Why make such a point of this?

Everything Jesus stands for is summed up in his calling God "Father" (*Abba*) and flows from his experience of intimacy with God expressed in this term of endearment. This is why "Son of God" expresses better than any other title not only his relationship to God, but also to us. He is "firstborn among many siblings" (Romans 8:29). Three concepts on which the Christian tradition hinges spring from Jesus' filial intimacy with God: Good News, Kingdom of God, and Salvation.

1. "Good News" is a term for the core teaching of Jesus, rooted in his experience of God as *Abba*, loving Father. The First Letter of John summarizes the Good News succinctly: "God is love, and all who abide in love abide in God, and God in them" (1 John 4:16).

2. "Kingdom of God" is the world—that part of the world which "abides in love." With the poet Gary Snyder, who speaks of the "Earth Household," we could call the Kingdom of God the "God Household." In speaking of a household here, we avoid the misunderstanding that Jesus merely replaced a secular domination system with a sacred one. On the contrary, he lived and died to overcome any form of domination system. Its total opposite is meant by "Kingdom of God." The Earth Household *is* the God Household—except for us humans. The God Household knows no unnecessary domination, no unjust oppression, and no selfish exploitation. Only we humans, like the Prodigal Son in the parable (Luke 15:11–32) who left home for "an alien land," have become alienated.

3. "Salvation" is homecoming. When love, not power, reigns supreme, alienation from ourselves, from all others, and from God is healed. The moment we realize we can never fall out of God's love, we "come to

ourselves" like the wayward son in the parable—to our true Self, at home in the God Household as a uniquely loved member of the family. And now we become catalysts for the salvation of the whole world, its transformation from power and domination to service and love. Salvation—and this needs to be stressed—is not a private matter.

All this is implied when we speak of Jesus Christ as GOD'S ONLY SON. We are by no means limiting ourselves to saying something about Jesus. Rather, we proclaim that every human being is a son or daughter of God. We commit ourselves to this all-inclusive family of God, and we accept our responsibility as members of the God Household. In this phrase of the Creed, which seems so innocuous at first sight, almost irrelevant to daily life, we confront issues of prime importance—human dignity, nonviolence, environmental stewardship. Our membership in the God Household demands from us action in all these areas.

Personal reflections

In my reflections on the previous section, JESUS CHRIST, I used one of Gerard Manley Hopkins's best-known sonnets, usually identified by its first words, "As kingfishers catch fire." This poem suggests that Christ-consciousness is a step up from self-consciousness (in the sense of self-awareness)—in Hopkins's words, from "selving" to "justicing." By making justice—fairness and harmony in all relationships within and without—his central concern, "the just man justices" and so "acts in God's eye what in God's eye he is—Christ."

Hopkins's imagery has helped me expand the narrow understanding of my grade-school days, when "Christ" was simply another name for Jesus. And if its first part can help us understand faith in Christ, its last three lines can help us understand faith in Christ as GOD'S ONLY SON:

for Christ plays in ten thousand places,
Lovely in limbs, and lovely in eyes not his
To the Father through the features of men's faces.

The idea that Christ "plays" picks up the image of a dancer that had been intimated in the preceding lines. Like Paul and John and other New Testament writers, Hopkins fuses here the image of Christ with that of Sophia, God's Wisdom personified, who at all times plays with delight before God (as we read in Proverbs 8:22–31, one of the loveliest passages in the Bible). But here the poet brings new depth of vision to this image. He sees—and this is the decisive point—Christ at play in limbs and eyes "not his." Christ becomes visible through the features of human faces, and this "in ten thousand places." Wherever we may be, the Lord of all becomes manifest in each and all of us. The Cosmic Christ plays "in" and "through" us in the Father's sight. Close your eyes and hold this image. Its message is clear. Faith in Jesus Christ as God's "only" son is not exclusive; it includes you and me in this singular relationship of love.

The poetry of Gerard Manley Hopkins is rich in imagery and tight in structure. This demands a certain effort from readers. But I trust that you will want to reread in its entirety the sonnet I have quoted so extensively, and that you will find your effort rewarded.

As kingfishers catch fire, dragonflies draw flame;
As tumbled over rim in roundy wells
Stones ring; like each tucked string tells, each hung bell's
Bow swung finds tongue to fling out broad its name;
Each mortal thing does one thing and the same:
Deals out that being indoors each one dwells;
Selves—goes itself; myself it speaks and spells,
Crying What I do is me: for that I came.

I say more: the just man justices;
Keeps grace: that keeps all his goings graces;

Acts in God's eye what in God's eye he is—
Christ—for Christ plays in ten thousand places,
Lovely in limbs, and lovely in eyes not his
To the Father through the features of men's faces.

What image in this poem speaks to you personally? How would you express the gist of the poet's message in your own words? What does "justicing" imply in your own daily life? How does the perspective of this section compare with other perspectives on Jesus Christ with which you are familiar?

Our Lord

~

What does this really mean?

Lord was the title of the Roman Emperor. For Christians to call Jesus LORD amounted to high treason. Only one could have ultimate authority. If Jesus is LORD, the Emperor is not. This calls for decision: Power or love? Empire or God Household? The nonviolent social revolution that Jesus Christ set in motion threatens the very foundations of every world order based on power, every empire, every oppressive system—political or religious—even if it gives itself a Christian veneer.

Long before the Roman emperor was called *lord*, this was God's title. The corresponding Greek word, *kyrios*, was used in the earliest translations of the Hebrew Scriptures (third century BCE) in place of the unspeakable Name of God. It pointed toward God's supreme power. Now, Jesus taught by word and deed that God's power was the power of love. Thus, when the early Christians said "God is love," they proclaimed the absolute, universal, and intimately personal authority of Love. They had experienced God's love personified, as it were, in Jesus Christ. Following him meant standing up with him in the power of love against any other power in the world. Because he represented that divine power, they could dare give him the title LORD, the title of the God whose power is love. We, today, can also experience in our heart of hearts the powerful claim of love as challenge to say—or rather live—our "Yes!" to belonging. This "Yes!" is unconditional and the belonging is unlimited. When we become aware of this authoritative claim of love within us, and recognize the same love embodied in Jesus Christ, it makes sense to call him LORD as representative of divine Love.

Faith in Jesus Christ as LORD means ultimate trust in the power of God's love shining forth in him. It implies facing up to the demands of such love by living accordingly. A world in which the sovereignty of love determines relationships and events is diametrically opposed to the alienated dog-eat-dog world we have created. The divine lordship of love will inevitably clash with the authoritarian claims of power structures in the world in which we live. Faith in Jesus Christ as OUR LORD implies courage to engage in this struggle. The OUR emphasizes the universality of the new world order of love. It includes not only Christians, but all for whom love is the ultimate authority.

How do we know this is so?

Understanding what LORD—Kyrios—means and what Jesus Christ stands for flows from a careful study of the Bible. Only in the context of the biblical tradition does the wording of the Creed make sense. The meaning of the Creed, however, goes far beyond its particular wording and its immediate context. By connecting its statements with our personal inner experience and deepest awareness, we can come to see their universal significance. Even a notion like the Lordship of Jesus Christ, which would otherwise appear irrelevant to all but Christians, becomes deeply meaningful to those who start not from the often-misunderstood claims of this particular religion, but from universal spiritual experience that is accessible to every human being.

In our peak moments we experience the bliss of limitless belonging. Our heart spontaneously says "Yes!" to this belonging. To stick to this "Yes!" in all the choices of life is the great challenge of love in the midst of an alienated world. On the basis of this experience of our own, we can come to recognize it also in Jesus and in all he represents. His "Yes!" to universal belonging finds expression in his way of teaching (in parables), in his key concept of the

Kingdom of God (the God Household), and in his understanding of God as loving Father (*Abba*). Jesus lived and died for the demands of love. Recognizing these demands in our own heart as the voice of divine authority, we can come to see that same divine authority embodied in Jesus Christ. Whether or not we are Christians, we can thus understand the meaning of "Jesus Christ is Lord" (Philippians 2:11).

Why make such a point of this?

Faith in Jesus Christ as OUR LORD finds expression in one's commitment to the ultimate authority of Love to which he bears witness in the world. Without this commitment, *Lord* is an empty title, but to make this faith commitment has vast practical implications. If divine love embodied in Jesus Christ is our ultimate authority, we will have to question the claims of all other authorities—respectfully, but no less radically.

Love is a "Yes!" to belonging and its radical expression in every aspect of life. Each one of us can and must work toward a world in which love is the ultimate authority. This "Yes!" to belonging is the Creative Power enlivening all of nature. No living creature can survive in isolation. Each is connected with all others by an intricate network of relationships. All are embedded in a shared matrix in which they mutually sustain one another. The whole evolves through the interaction of all its parts. A closer look at any field, hedgerow, or plot of wetland will show us the "Yes!" to belonging in action. We need only allow this power, which is so obvious in nature, to flow also into human culture.

What is true of a forest is also true of any society: no living creature can survive in isolation. But we have the choice: we can gratefully cultivate the relationships that make us part of a vast network, or we can take them for granted and allow them to wither and die. Like any rain forest, a culture evolves and thrives through the interaction of all its members. But as humans we need to plug into the creative power that achieves this marvelous unfolding by saying our willing "Yes!" to belonging. Christian tradition calls this Creative Power "the Holy Spirit"—the "Creator Spirit." "But the fruit of the Spirit is love, joy, peace, patience, kindness, goodness, faithfulness, gentleness, self-control" (Galatians 5:22–23). Imagine a society that brings forth fruit of this kind.

"No one can say 'Jesus is Lord' except in the Holy Spirit," asserts Saint Paul (I Corinthians 12:3). Therefore the next section of the Creed will speak of Jesus Christ as "conceived by the Holy Spirit."

Personal reflections

Michelangelo's *Pietá* is the best-known representation of the Sorrowful Mother, Mary, holding one last time the body of her crucified son. Again and again, artists have depicted this scene with great tenderness, and the sorrow of countless mothers in mourning made these images greatly beloved by popular piety. Our parish church in Vienna housed, in a special chapel, a wood-carved statue of the Sorrowful Mother, and every year on the Friday before Good Friday thousands of pilgrims came to pray there. In 1944 the road leading up to our church saw on that Friday of Sorrows a never-ending stream of women in black, bewailing the slaughter of their sons and grandsons who had been forced into the army as cannon fodder for Hitler's wars. Only a handful of them could have known that three days before, in a neighboring church, a young priest had been arrested by the Gestapo on charges of high treason, precisely because he had taken a stand against this insane enslavement and killing of millions.

The priest's name was Heinrich Maier. He was the kind of chaplain whom students like me loved and admired. While he had been celebrating the Eucharist that morning, three men entered the church and took position in front of the altar, arms folded and legs spread. This defiant posture was all the congregation got to see, but immediately after the priest left the altar and entered the sacristy, the three men arrested him, still wearing the sacred vestments, and took him away. Lisi Irdinger, the brave and clever helper at the rectory, rushed to Father Maier's room, grabbed his papers, and put them in the room of chaplain Robert Firneis. This priest had been drafted into the army, and so his room was exempt from searching by the Gestapo. Informers, however, had told the authorities all they needed to know: this bright young cleric, with two doctor titles to his name at age thirty-four, beloved by those whom he served, had founded a group within the Austrian Resistance, had taken up contact with similar groups in Germany, especially with members of Catholic unions, and was even in touch with the Secret Service of the Allies. He had tried to limit indiscriminate bombing of civilian targets by helping to direct Allied air strikes toward armament factories. All this was certainly enough for the verdict of treason and the sentence of death by beheading.

On the Friday of Mary's Sorrows in the following year, the flow of pilgrims up the valley between the vineyards was merely a trickle. By now, bombardments had turned whole districts of Vienna into fields of rubble. Though the liberating Russian army was approaching from the Hungarian border, and the end of Hitler's "Thousand-Year Reich" was in sight, maybe the worst was still to come. Still, as we put it at that time, "Better an end with horror than horror without end." The reign of terror was indeed collapsing. We did not yet know it, but the preceding day, the twenty-second of March, 1945, had been the day on which the guillotine in the dreaded prison downtown had done its bloody work for the last time. It had stopped for good, but one of the last heads to fall on that day had been Father Heinrich Maier's.

When I think of him now, what I remember is fused with what I learned later: that he was tied, naked, to the window grating in prison and tortured; that, even under torture, he did not betray a single one of his co-conspirators; that a cynical judge, impressed by his steadfast courage, asked, "If you take all the blame upon yourself, what do you get for it?" and got the answer, "I will not need much from now on." I remember that many said, "Well, he stuck his neck out, so he got his head chopped off. What else did he expect?"

I remember also, it was from heroes like Heinrich Maier that I learned what it means to confess Jesus Christ as *Lord*. He did so with a loud voice, fellow prisoners reported, moments before he was silenced forever.

You and I can still speak up. We still have necks to stick out. When did *we* last stand up against injustice? Hitler was neither the first nor the last to start a war of aggression, sell it to his people by lies, and keep it going through a propaganda of fear. Millions of women are weeping for their children cut down in the prime of life—today as then. Will the sorrow of mothers arouse us? For whom will we stick out our necks—for the warlords, or for the LORD of justice and peace?

Conceived by the Holy Spirit

◆

What does this really mean?

Note that CONCEIVED BY THE HOLY SPIRIT is a statement about the *adult* Jesus, the Christ, which is here projected back into his origins. It wants to say: with Jesus Christ, a divine life-power—the Holy Spirit—breaks through the dead encrustations of history. This is expressed in the mythic image of conception. It needs to be stressed, however, that the image is taken from Hebrew rather than from Greek mythology. This makes a great difference. The Creed is rooted in the biblical mind. Thus, the idea that Jesus could be conceived in a similar way as, say, the Greek demigod Perseus, whom Zeus sired by pouring a golden shower on his mother, Danae, would be considered blasphemy.

The biblical reference point for conception BY THE HOLY SPIRIT is the creation story in the first book of Moses. There the Spirit of God hovers like a mother bird over the waters of chaos and hatches an ordered cosmos (Genesis 1:2). Later in this story, God takes material from this cosmos and shapes it into a human body; then God breathes the Holy Spirit—God's own Life-breath—into the nostrils of this figure, "and so the Earthling became a living being" (Genesis 2:7). Against this background, the image of Jesus' conception BY THE HOLY SPIRIT signifies that the life we encounter in him is God's Life-breath filling the universe and making each one of us alive; but what we know as a spark of divine life within ourselves we see in Jesus Christ fully ablaze.

When we call God's Spirit *Holy*, we do not point to moral perfection, but to religious awe. *Holy* in this sense is not an ethical term but a spiritual one. It refers to the awe-inspiring power of divine life and love breaking through layers of human coldness—personal as well as institutional—and we recognize it as God's concept realized in and through Jesus Christ.

How do we know this is so?

THE HOLY SPIRIT as the awe-inspiring power of life and of love is a reality with which every human being is familiar, whatever name we give to it. SPIRIT is the very aliveness of our life. This holds true for every one of us. We differ only by the degree to which we open ourselves to this power. Fear tends to block and close our access to "life in fullness" (John 10:10) for which Jesus Christ stands. Life is always a gradual process, however, and we must respect the pace of its movement. The seed needs time to grow. If we patiently cultivate courage and openness, we will become more and more aware of the SPIRIT within us that allows us to know God, love God, and thrive in God, because this power quickens our intellect, our will, and our emotions.

There is also a way in which we can make sense of the idea that Jesus Christ was CONCEIVED BY THE HOLY SPIRIT. We can think of his life as conceived in the mind of God similar to the way the hero of a story is conceived in the storyteller's mind. A poetic understanding of this sort comes much closer to the mind-set of the Gospel writers than to the literalism of later interpreters. It has well been said that we must choose between taking the Gospels seriously or literally. If we read them with a sense for poetry, we will not be able to dodge their serious challenge. We will be moved by the strength and tenderness, the revolutionary fervor and fervent pacifism of the towering figure of Jesus alive with the very Life-breath of God. Then all that is best in us will be stirred not only by his example, but by the stirring of his very SPIRIT within us. Yes, this SPIRIT is in us all; it is the very life of our life. For all this unfolding reality in us and around us is a story of love, CONCEIVED by God in the SPIRIT of love.

Why make such a point of this?

What makes CONCEIVED BY THE HOLY SPIRIT so important a clause is this: it places the Creed squarely within the perennial tradition of mystic spirituality. The Creed introduces here THE HOLY SPIRIT, without any further explanation of that term. It presupposes we know from experience what we are talking about. Thus it links the profession of faith with the experience of knowing, loving, and enjoying God in our hearts. But this is mystical life—the awareness of God's life within us.

The Creed anticipates here the later clause, "I believe in the Holy Spirit," and so implies faith in God as "triune"—"Father," the ultimate mystery from whom we come and to whom we are on our way; "Son," in whom we find our true Self; "Spirit," the divine aliveness within our own innermost life. Here we touch upon the very core of faith.

The phrase CONCEIVED BY THE HOLY SPIRIT expresses implicitly our trust in the breakthrough of the divine Spirit that happened in history through Jesus Christ, say, when he touched the untouchables, sat down at table with the outcasts, gave women equal status with men. It implies our commitment to the spiritual struggle that this breakthrough has set in motion throughout the centuries and up to our own time; think of Dorothy Day and her witness for peace; of Cesar Chavez, who restored dignity to exploited farm workers; of Mother Teresa, who served the poorest of the poor. This phrase of the Creed is not about a piece of (unverifiable) genetic information concerning Jesus. Rightly understood, it ties together mystic vision and resolute action in the world. How else did the Antislavery Movement come about, the Civil Rights Movement, the Women's Liberation Movement, Gay Liberation, any peace movement, and the global ecology movement? How did these movements come about if not CONCEIVED BY THE HOLY SPIRIT? These words of the Creed become the proclamation of our own dynamic relationship to the Spirit. By pronouncing them we make a commitment to carry out what the Spirit conceived and what Jesus bore witness to by his life and death.

Personal reflections

The concept of connectedness can help us understand the workings of the Holy Spirit in the world. Yet we should not expect too much from a concept; it can at best lead to an intellectual appreciation. True understanding flows only from personal experience. Since we experience connections uninterruptedly in everything we do, we tend to take them for granted. After all, everything is connected with everything else. It helps, therefore, to focus on moments when, unexpectedly, a surprising connection catches our attention. For example, in moments of what C. G. Jung termed *synchronicity*, connections flare up.

You can, most likely, remember synchronistic experiences of your own. Just to prime the pump, let me relate one of many I can remember. In the 1990s I had the privilege of lecturing at Schumacher College, located in Devon. This southwestern part of England is a delightful region for hiking. Since I happened to have two consecutive days off, William Thomas, a staff member with whom I had become friends, offered to be my guide through the wild and glorious upland area of Dartmoor National Park.

As we were walking side by side through this landscape of stark and barren beauty, we talked about many things, and the topic of synchronicity came up. William told me of a teacher from India who worked in the streets of London with "broken" people, as he put it. Now, William collects terms for "butterfly" in different languages—*mariposa, farfalla, Schmetterling, papillon*—and so he asked that teacher what a butterfly was called in the local dialect with which he grew up in India. "Well," the man answered, "I haven't spoken my native language in a long time, but let me see— butterfly, butterfly?" At that moment, William told me, as if called by its name, a butterfly appeared as if out of nowhere there in the city and alighted on the teacher's chest. Moreover, this butterfly had a broken wing, as if in connection with the "broken" people so close to the teacher's heart.

It sounded to me like an impressive instance of synchronicity, but what happened while William was telling me about it was still more striking. We had not seen many butterflies, if any, on our two-day hike, but while he was speaking about that butterfly, I noticed one fluttering toward us. At the moment William was saying, "and the butterfly alighted on his chest," this one was directly in front of me and—"No, no, that cannot be real!" I screamed inside myself—it alighted on my heart.

Connection was a key concept also in Thomas Merton's theological thought. He was deeply aware that in the Holy Spirit everything is connected with everything. We spent time together at Redwoods Monastery in northern California shortly before his trip to the Far East, from which he was never to return. The topic of connections had been prominent in our conversations, and now Merton was celebrating the Eucharist in the monastery chapel. The wall behind the altar was all glass and opened onto a redwood grove. Shafts of sunlight sifted through the branches of the ancient trees. The Gospel that day spoke of the Kingdom of God as the Great Wedding Feast. Little did we anticipate the surprising way the connection between this Gospel and our natural surroundings would soon be brought home to us—the connection between liturgy and instinctive behavior, between a human ritual and a ritual of insects. At communion time, an amazing spectacle caught our eyes. Perfectly synchronized with our communion procession, another procession took place outside the window. It was a procession of flying ants—thousands of tiny, glittering wings across the forest glade.

In moments like this we wake up to the miracle of connectedness, but even when we are not awake to it, a marvelous interweaving of all things and events is constantly going on. Because God is love, and love is the Yes to belonging, God's HOLY SPIRIT is the power that animates the deepest belonging of all to all. Jesus stood up for love, belonging, and connectedness in the power of the HOLY SPIRIT, and so his life—from his very conception—can be understood as CONCEIVED BY THE HOLY SPIRIT, as the realization in history of something that God, beyond time, CONCEIVED.

The Spirit's concept of history is not a blueprint, but rather an inspiration and an invitation to improvise. The Gospel story of the Annunciation makes this point quite clearly, for it implies that the Yes that Mary said did make a difference in God's plan. Connections conceived by the Holy Spirit are not mechanical, like interlocking wheels in a clockwork; they are much more like the bonds we celebrate at a wedding feast. When we establish connections of love and friendship, of solidarity and caring, we can feel the Spirit's power pulsating through our hearts. In those moments we get an inkling of what kind of world God has conceived and wants us to realize in the power of the Spirit. Jesus glimpsed God's concept of the world. He called it God's Kingdom. By focusing our human efforts on cultivating tender connections and caring relationships, we can give birth to such a world CONCEIVED BY THE HOLY SPIRIT.

And you? Have you ever experienced a connectedness that seemed to call for an expansion of our too-narrow worldview? (In my reflections above, I have used an example of this kind—synchronicity—to point to a still deeper connectedness of all with all by THE HOLY SPIRIT.) When you read Jesus' infancy stories in the Gospels according to Matthew and Luke as wanting to tell us something about the *adult* Christ, do you feel enriched, or deprived of a simpler approach dear to you, or maybe a little of both? Who, besides Jesus, comes to mind when you think of THE HOLY SPIRIT breaking through the layers of human coldness? (Think not only of the saints of different traditions, but of great artists, statesmen, scientists, and musicians.) Are you familiar with popular movements (facilitated maybe by the Internet) that seem to you CONCEIVED BY THE HOLY SPIRIT?

Born of the Virgin Mary

~

What does this really mean?

In short, BORN OF THE VIRGIN MARY means that the birth of Jesus Christ—in the world as well as in hearts that trust in him—marks the dew-fresh dawn of a new beginning. Virgin birth is a mythic image for an altogether new start.

"Mythic?" someone is apt to ask. "Do you mean this doctrine is not true?" On the contrary. A mythic image conveys far more truth than an abstract statement—as long as we do not take it literally. If the phrase BORN OF THE VIRGIN MARY were a gynecological report, then the sentence "I give you my heart" would have to refer to a heart transplant. In both cases we are dealing with poetic language. No other way of speaking can pack so much meaning into so few words. This is why we wax poetic when we are in love. Poetry can carry a great deal more truth than reporting. Myth is the expression of insights too weighty for any but poetic language.

In a society operating at a level of consciousness in which mythic tales are not distinguished from reports of historic events, no one will have a problem declaring Jesus was BORN OF THE VIRGIN MARY. On a more sophisticated level of understanding, this statement is still taken as true, but now people make a distinction between myths and facts, and reject mythical stories as not having happened literally the way they are told. Only on yet the next level of consciousness does the insight dawn, that myths contain truth. This deeper truth reveals itself only when we do not take myths literally. Those who step up to this level are able to deal constructively with clashes between the teachings of different traditions.

They can see that vastly different stories may convey a similar message. This is of prime importance for interreligious dialogue.

Of course, not all members of a social group are on the same level of development. Schools could make a decisive contribution to religious tolerance by fostering an appreciation of poetry. We have a crying need for a school system in which the cultivation of a poetic mind ranks high. A sense for poetry is indispensable for the understanding of myths.

How do we know this is so?

If the statement that Jesus was conceived and born of a virgin were to be taken as a physiological report, it simply could not be verified. Any attempt to understand it in this sense collapses as soon as we ask, "How do you know?" As mythical image, however, virgin birth carries a clear and weighty message: here and now a momentous new beginning is taking place. Mythmakers have invented a great many variations on this theme. A virgin may be impregnated by a sunray; she may swallow a pebble and give birth to Stone Boy, a rock of a man; she may conceive in her dream; a god may make her a mother by letting a shower of gold rain down on her, or an angel may ask her consent (what respect for human dignity!) to give birth to God's son.

To understand these images in the way they were meant, we must develop a sense for poetic language, the language of myth. Mythic images speak to our intellect through our poetic sensibility, and this sensibility needs to be cultivated. This presupposes a certain degree of maturity. In puberty the young person rejects fairy tales as lies; only later does their deeper truth dawn on the mind. To understand the Creed, the Bible, or any of humanity's sacred writings, one needs to tune in to the language of myth. This tuning-in means both taking them seriously and not taking them literally.

In the sense in which we speak of virginal snow where no skier has as yet left tracks, or of a virginal page in a new blank book, *virginal* can also stand for unprejudiced receptivity. Experience teaches us that encountering new and significant ideas demands an inner attitude that is unprejudiced in its receptivity and motherly in its nourishing care for an embryonic insight. A similar attitude characterizes the most fruitful attitude toward people we meet on an intimate level. When a friend receives you with an accepting, caring heart, you begin to conceive of yourself in a new way, and your genuine Self unfolds. In this way, true friends become mothers to each other. Thus we can know a deeper meaning of "virgin birth," one that can be verified from personal experience and makes a difference in daily life.

Why make such a point of this?

To be relevant enough for its place in the Creed, BORN OF THE VIRGIN MARY must have a significance that goes far beyond its literal meaning. A brief summary of what it wants to say may run like this: Faith in God (and the Creed is concerned with nothing else) takes a historic turn through Jesus Christ, and this new spirituality demands from us a virginally new readiness to receive it. The key word is *Newness*.

All right, but couldn't all this be said more directly? Couldn't it be expressed in imagery more accessible to people in the third millennium than the archaic myth of virgin birth? The answer to these questions is a decisive "Yes!" So why hold on to the formula BORN OF THE VIRGIN MARY? The answer here will depend on our understanding of what "holding on" means in this context. There are many ways of holding on, from the desperate clinging of a drowning swimmer to a lifesaving plank, to the playful lightness with which dancers hold each other in a ballet. To me, the most fitting way of holding on to the words and images of the Creed is the delicate firmness with which an archer holds on to an arrow at the moment of letting go. With these words and images we aim at an understanding that we can reach only if we combine with refined sensitivity both the holding and the letting go.

For private use, I would recommend to all who read this book to write down their personal creed in their own words. One might repeat this exercise on every birthday. Should we not expect our faith to grow, to ripen, and to be changed through life's experience, yet remain the same? After all, our bodies remain the same throughout life, and yet every single cell is changed and renewed. To make rewriting our personal creed an element of our private birthday celebrations could help us understand ever more deeply what the Franciscan priest Father Richard Rohr puts so well: "God comes to you disguised in your life." To the eyes of faith this is obvious. Our life situation is continually changing; our life is anchored in the unchanging Now of God's presence.

To reformulate our personal faith again and again is not only justified, but necessary. Why, then, not do the same with the official Creed we recite in church? My counterquestion: Why still light candles in an age of electric light? The candle flames reflected in our eyes as we sit around a festive table are the flames of fires around which our forebears sat a hundred thousand years before us. On festive occasions we humans tend to hold on to traditional forms. Thus, on festive occasions it means something to me to profess my faith in the words and images that were venerable to my Christian forebears throughout the centuries. In the Creed they have handed on to me a text made venerable through its origin, its history, and its worldwide distribution. For better or worse, I have made it my task to understand this text, not to replace it. In doing so, I found that this venerable text became transparent and so even more venerable. Its statements of belief became transparent to the faith which they express. And while the beliefs belong only to Christians, the underlying faith is the most precious heirloom of every child born into this world; it unites us and makes us human.

Why should we give up the BORN OF THE VIRGIN MARY on account of those who take it literally and so affirm or deny it based on a misunderstanding? At every moment eternity bursts into time. The image of the virgin birth allows us to celebrate this ever-new beginning in an irreplaceable poetic form that speaks not only to the head, but also to the heart.

There is a further reason that it is worth making a point of BORN OF THE VIRGIN MARY, maybe the most cogent reason today. Behind the image of the virgin birth stands the image of the Annunciation in the Gospel according to Luke (chapter 1). There Mary is invited to say a free Yes to the invitation to participate in the plan God conceived. Luke portrays the Virgin Mary as a woman free to decide whether she wants to conceive and give birth in the world to the Word of God. What Luke projects here from the life of the adult Jesus into his origins is revolutionary: he gave to women equal status with men. And there is more to it. From the beginning, women—independently of men—were responsive to God's message as Jesus proclaimed it, and gave it tangible form in the world around them. How many oppressed and exploited women throughout history must have found solace and strength in this passage of the Creed? It can still give us courage and hope in the struggle of women against power structures in the Church and in the world at large. This, to me, is a point worth stressing.

Personal reflections

It strikes me as remarkable that popular piety has focused on one scene in the Virgin Mary's life more than on all others together: the Annunciation. In Christian art, the image of Mary's encounter with the Archangel Gabriel, as recounted in the first chapter of Luke's Gospel, has been a favorite motif, century after century. Anyone traveling in Europe will find it at every turn, in churches, in museums, in wayside shrines, and on the walls of houses. More striking still: morning, noon, and evenings, church bells will ring in every village, town, and city to commemorate Gabriel's message to Mary and her response. The Angelus, as this prayer is called, represents the Christian parallel to the sacred prayer times in Islam and in other traditions. At three crucial points of the day—when night turns to morning, at the turning point of high noon, and when evening turns into night—the Angelus prayer celebrates the breaking of eternity into time, and reminds us to live in the Now.

The traditional form of the Angelus is simple. Three short verses, together repeated at each prayer time, constitute its core. "The angel of the Lord brought the message to Mary, and she conceived by the Holy Spirit." This first verse sets the scene. The second one quotes from the Gospel and invites us to make Mary's response our own: "Behold, the handmaid of the Lord; be it done to me according to your word." And the third verse—this one from the Prologue to John's Gospel—spells out what happened then and is to happen now if we are responsive and receptive like Mary: "The Word was made flesh and came to dwell among us." These three verses are woven together by a threefold recitation of the Hail Mary, itself composed for the most part of Gabriel's words to Mary.

Having learned this prayer as a small child, I can testify to its power to give a stable structure to the day, and to bring me back, in spite of all the ups and downs of time, to the Now. When should the Word become flesh, if not now? How should this happen, if not by my opening myself to the Spirit? And what could bring more momentous a change to my life and to the world around me? At the sound of the bells, the Angelus prayer ritualizes the story of the Annunciation and thus allows its life-giving power to flow into our lives. To pray not only when we feel like praying, but *when it is time*, when the bell rings, this attunes our lives to the cosmic rhythm of times and seasons. It grounds us in the greater reality supporting our minute existence.

From my early grade-school days I remember once looking down from an upper window onto the walkways between the school's buildings. Just then, the Angelus bell rang out from the church steeple. Every movement stopped. It looked from high up as if the bustling movement of an anthill on a summer day's high noon had suddenly come to a standstill. But this was not a dead silence, it was a life-giving one, like the silence of the village smith when he stopped to take a deep breath.

And I remember a festive day in the early 1980s, when Bernie Glassman Roshi, a Zen teacher whom I admire for his deep social commitment, was being ordained as abbot of Greystone Mandala in New York. Zen teachers from far away had come for this ritual. Their gorgeous golden robes, the arrangements of chrysanthemums, the many candles, and the clouds of incense reminded me vividly of a solemn High Mass in a Catholic or Anglican cathedral—best of all, the sacred silence between chants. Into this silence, suddenly the beeper on someone's wristwatch went off. Oops! One couldn't help but feel sorry for the unfortunate owner of that jinxed timepiece. But Bernie Glassman spoke up and announced, "This was my alarm. I have taken a vow to interrupt whatever I am doing at high noon and to think thoughts of peace. Please join me for a moment in doing so. Our world needs it."

And you? Do you make time to stop and breathe deeply? Have you built into your day moments when you stop time in its tracks? The world needs our conscious effort again and again to return to the Now in virginal receptivity for the creative power of the Spirit.

Suffered Under Pontius Pilate

What does this really mean?

It means, first of all, we are dealing with hard reality here. In the two preceding statements we did so, too, but it was less obvious because they were couched in poetic language. This one reminds us that our faith is anchored in fact—in historically datable events. Putting metaphor and reportage side by side like this has an almost comical effect, as in the sentence, "The moon, smiling confidante of secret lovers, circles Earth at an average distance of 238,900 miles." Here in the Creed, the juxtaposition serves a purpose: it reminds us, both ways of speaking must be taken lightly, they point beyond themselves.

SUFFERED UNDER PONTIUS PILATE pins down a historical fact, yet, as such, a historical fact has no justification for being mentioned here. After all, the Creed is not an enumeration of facts that Christians hold to be true, but a multifaceted profession of faith in God—its one and only theme—that is reformulated in each of its statements from a different perspective. How then does Pontius Pilate suddenly pop up in the Creed?

We can find the answer to this question by noticing the tension between this phrase and the previous one, between virgin birth and Passion. This tension is vital for the life of faith and an understanding of the two poles of life in the Spirit. This phrase draws our attention to opposite poles: there, the woman who gives life, here, the man who kills; there, the vulnerable virgin, here, the powerful politician; there, a new beginning in the power of the Spirit, here, its destruction by the spirit of power. Because Jesus stands for God's world order he must clash with an upside-down disorder that calls itself order. In this collision, however, he suffers shipwreck.

Everyone knows Einstein's famous equation $E = mc^2$, but he is also credited with a less famous one: $a = x+y+z$. "If a stands for success," Einstein is said to have explained, "x stands for effort, y stands for relaxation, and z stands for keeping your mouth shut." Jesus did not follow this pragmatic advice. What he conceived in silence through the Holy Spirit he proclaimed aloud through word and deed. All those whose faith in God finds expression in their faith in Jesus Christ who SUFFERED UNDER PONTIUS PILATE must realize what they are in for. Citizens, for instance, who demonstrate against the use of torture by their government take the kind of stance that Jesus took. They commit themselves to speak up for justice and compassion and peace, as the Spirit guides them—like Jesus "who made the good profession under Pontius Pilate" (1 Timothy 6:13) and sealed his witnessing with his lifeblood.

To mention Pontius Pilate by name in the Creed means I know who the top dogs of this world are—then and now; I know them by name, and I know what suffering they can inflict on those who speak up; and yet I put my ultimate trust in Jesus Christ the underdog. It means I know what happened to him and is likely to happen in one way or another to his true followers, and yet, I commit myself, as the Quakers do, "to speak truth to power."

How do we know this is so?

The outer reality affirmed here—the fact that Jesus suffered under a representative of the Roman Empire, named Pontius Pilate, who governed Judea from 26 to 36 CE—is subject to historical verification. More scholarly research has been done on this subject in our time than in all previous centuries, and the positive results are available to a general readership. (A book that draws out the historical perspectives of Jesus' passion is *The Last Week: What the Gospels Really Teach About Jesus's Final Days in Jerusalem* by M. J. Borg and J. D. Crossan.)

The inner reality of the clash between Jesus Christ and Pontius Pilate becomes accessible to us when we compare two sets of values—those of the Kingdom of God, as Jesus proclaimed it, and those of every domination system in history; values like compassion, beauty, and truth, that we experience in our most alive moments—our peak experiences—and the values (or lack of values) by which the world we have created is for the most part run. (Here, too, I would recommend a small book that has become a classic, Abraham Maslow's *Peak Experiences, Values and Religion*.)

Daily experience shows us how difficult it is to stand up for those spiritual values to which we feel committed when we are at our best. Whenever we have to swim against the current for the sake of our deepest convictions, we know why Jesus SUFFERED UNDER PONTIUS PILATE. The second letter to Titus states a truth that remains as valid today as it was in New Testament times: "Indeed, all who wish to live God-loving lives in Jesus Christ will suffer persecution" (2 Titus 3:12).

Gandhi, Martin Luther King, Cesar Chavez, Rosa Parks, Dorothy Day, Karen Silkwood, the Desaparecidos of Latin American dictatorships who were secretly abducted and killed for standing up for basic human rights, and countless others—victims, all of them, of the power represented in the Creed by Pontius Pilate.

Why make such a point of this?

When the Creed asserts that Jesus SUFFERED UNDER PONTIUS PILATE, it not only points to "everything that Jesus taught and *did*" (Acts 1:1), but also, and importantly, what happened to him on account of it. This is important because it shows us the cost of discipleship—the price Jesus had to pay for the stand he took, and therefore the price any of us must be prepared to pay who take a stand with him.

This passage of the Creed forms a unit with the two preceding ones. Together they spell out what life as God's children demands from us: to be led by God's Holy Spirit, to give birth to Christ in our world, and to bear the terrifying yet glorious consequences.

1. Jesus was CONCEIVED BY THE HOLY SPIRIT and "led by the Spirit" (Matthew 4:1), and "*all* who are led by the Spirit of God are sons and daughters of God" (Romans 8:14).

2. BORN OF THE VIRGIN MARY, Jesus came into the world, yet, long before that event, and ever after throughout history, God's Word is made flesh wherever humans courageously say "Yes," as Mary did, to the Spirit that "blows where it wishes" (John 3:8). "The anxious longing of the creation waits eagerly for the revealing of the sons of God. . . . For we know that the whole creation groans and suffers the pains of childbirth together until now" (Romans 8:19 and 22).

3. The suffering of Jesus under Pontius Pilate was part of these pains of birth, just as "all who wish to live God-loving lives in Jesus Christ will suffer persecution" (2 Titus 3:12). But with the apostle Paul they can say, "I rejoice in my sufferings . . . I do my share . . . in filling up what is lacking in Christ's afflictions" (Colossians 1:24). All suffering is part of one grand process. Eckhart Tolle put it succinctly: "You are here to enable the divine purpose of the universe to unfold." Suffering—as birth pangs—is necessary for the unfolding of that unimaginably glorious purpose. "The sufferings of this present time are not worthy to be compared with the glory that is to be revealed to us" (Romans 8:18).

A further reason this point is worth making: SUFFERED UNDER PONTIUS PILATE anchors transcendent reality firmly in history. For us, no less than for Jesus, history is the stage on which our spiritual convictions are put to the test. Jesus was executed by a representative of the domination system that is as powerful now as it was then. By putting, nevertheless, our faith in him we express our trust that the weakness of God is stronger than human power (1 Corinthians 1:25). Twenty-five centuries ago, the Taoist sage

Lao-tzu of ancient China expressed the same insight (without using God-language) in the words of the *Tao Te Ching*: "Nothing in the world is as soft and yielding as water. Yet for dissolving the hard and inflexible, nothing can surpass it. The weak overcomes the powerful; the gentle overcomes the rigid. Everyone knows this is true, but few can put it into practice" (chapter 78). Those who do put this principle into practice are men and women of faith. How could they do so without authentic faith, without courageous trust in an ultimate faithfulness at the core of reality? Jesus and Paul trusted in that faithfulness as the faithfulness of God. What matters, however, is faith, not the name we give to the reference point of that faith, for that is ultimately unnamable anyway.

Those who trust that "the weak overcomes the powerful; the gentle overcomes the rigid," may not see this truth verified by outward success; Jesus did not; neither did Paul. Still, they will say with Paul, "When I am weak, then I am strong" (2 Corinthians 12:10) and that very conviction will give them more inner strength than any tyrant can muster. History has shown this when Joan of Arc or Giordano Bruno perished in the flames kindled by the Inquisition and when Etty Hillesum or Edith Stein died in Nazi concentration camps—utterly weak, yet infinitely stronger than those who killed them. History is still showing it, for we may be sure that on this very day the Christ is suffering somewhere under some Pontius Pilate.

Thus, this passage of the Creed has a significance that goes far deeper than its literal sense. That Jesus had to suffer can give courage to all who in the midst of suffering remain faithful to their vision of a healed and whole and holy world.

Personal reflections

The reference to Pontius Pilate is essential, as it specifies precisely the kind of suffering the Creed is speaking about. It is the suffering inflicted by the powers dominating our world upon all who struggle for liberation. This was the suffering of Jesus, and it remains the quintessential suffering of those who follow him throughout the ages. But the domination system is only the most obvious expression of the kind of world we create when we forget our true Self and identify with our little ego in its alienation. Liberation from this alienation means the end of suffering. Compassion guides those who have attained liberation to share the pain of others in their struggle for liberation from alienation. These are the Bodhisattvas who turn back from the threshold of bliss in order to help all others to attain that same bliss. No matter how deep their compassion descends into suffering, it stays bright with the joy they have already tasted. This is where the archetypes of the Christ and the Bodhisattva meet.

For many who have had the privilege of getting to know His Holiness the Dalai Lama, he is the embodiment of the Bodhisattva ideal. I had this privilege for the first time when he met with a small group at Green Gulch Zen Center near San Francisco. One member in the group used this opportunity to play off the Buddhist tradition against the Christian one. "Buddhists teach us so well how to overcome suffering," he said. "What does Your Holiness have to say to Christians who for two thousand years have been wallowing in pain?" (This was only the gist of the question, but I did memorize the answer verbatim.) "Well, we must remember," the Dalai Lama replied, "according to Buddhist teaching, suffering is not overcome by leaving pain behind; suffering is overcome by bearing pain for others." In so brief a statement this great teacher managed to express a conviction shared by both Buddhists and Christians.

Whatever your own background, can you remember in your life an example of pain borne with so much love that suffering was overcome? Mothers will remember childbirth; teachers may recall how much heartache can be overcome when we bear it out of love for our students. Do you remember pictures of civil rights demonstrators in Selma, Alabama, knocked down by the blast of fire hoses and snapped at by police dogs? Have you ever taken part in some public demonstration for peace and justice or for some other cause? Where have you personally seen (for instance, on the evening news) the Christ suffer under some Pontius Pilate?

Crucified

~

What does this really mean?

The crucifixion of Jesus demonstrates that the Roman occupying power of first-century Israel considered him politically dangerous. Capital punishment for religious offenders was not normally crucifixion but stoning to death. The political as well as the religious powers of his time considered the teachings of Jesus as incendiary, and his actions as insurrectionary. If the Kingdom of God—so central to his message in word and deed—had been no more than an otherworldly ideal, he would certainly not have been executed for the sake of it. His crucifixion by the joint efforts of the Jewish Sanhedrin and the Roman governor shows that both religious and political authorities considered Jesus subversive.

All this is a matter of knowledge rather than faith. If CRUCIFIED was considered worthy to be mentioned in the Creed, a solemn profession of faith, there must be more to it than historical information. Every sentence of the Creed deals with one and the same theme: faith in God. What, then, is the implication of Jesus' crucifixion for this faith?

In order to answer this question we have to go back to the weighty AND by which the Creed includes faith in Jesus Christ within faith in God. This inclusion was possible only because human life can become transparent to the life of God, and did so in Jesus Christ. Thus, when we profess that God's tangible (1 John 1:1) presence in the world was CRUCIFIED, we express our faith that we can encounter God in the most horrible fate. In the midst of crucifixion—a scene seemingly screaming out God's absence—God is present. When we recite the word CRUCIFIED in the Creed, we have the opportunity to become aware that there is never anything so terrible in life or death as to prevent us from walking into it with trust in God's presence—no injustice, no pain, no catastrophe in and through which we cannot encounter God. This has given to countless men and women of faith a sense of peace and shelteredness in the midst of their darkest hours.

The plain CRUCIFIED distinguishes this earliest Creed from later ones that add "for us," or "on account of our sins." This implies that faith as we proclaim it here is open to a variety of possible interpretations of the crucifixion; it is not fixated on any one of them. We will see later how important this last point is.

How do we know this is so?

Historians inform us about the practice of crucifixion under Roman law. It was the capital punishment for rebellious slaves and for insurgents against Roman occupation. It was a punishment reserved for capital crimes against the order imposed by Rome's political authority. Jesus' death on a cross is a well-attested historical fact.

But what made Jesus so politically dangerous? It was his radical religious stance. Sam Keen says it succinctly: "Radical religion, as opposed to cultural religion, is always revolutionary." Radical religion is concerned with right living as much as with right teaching; it is concerned with social justice as much as with personal integrity; it makes a constant effort to tune in to God's guidance. Jesus' vision of a society that uses God's guidance as a plumb line—he called it the Kingdom of God—was diametrically opposed to the society in which he found himself, in which the privileged few exploited the masses of the poor. He shared table fellowship with outcasts, touched untouchable lepers, treated children and women with the same respect as men. His glance looked through the social ego of people straight to everyone's shining Self. Thus he restored social as well as spiritual dignity to the oppressed. He made them stand up. This is the reason that so many of the miracle stories describe him as making the lame stand on their own feet. And this is the reason also that he was called a rabble-rouser.

Jesus stood in the tradition of the Hebrew prophets. Their radical religion had always clashed with the official religion into which one must buy by giving up thinking for oneself. Jesus made people think for themselves; we know this from those Gospel texts that, by scholarly consensus, have the strongest claim for proximity to Jesus' own teaching, the parables. The typical parable of Jesus works like a joke. It starts with a familiar description and leads to a question—for instance, who of you does not know how it goes when one bakes bread with sourdough? Who of you does not know how a shepherd acts who loses a sheep, or a woman who loses a treasured coin? Who of you does not know what to do when finding good and bad fish in the same net, weeds among one's wheat, or a hidden treasure? Or when a long-lost wayward son returns home? The answer to these questions is always the same: Everybody knows. It's common sense. And then comes the implied clincher: If you know it so well in your day-by-day living, why don't you draw the consequences where your relationship with God is concerned? Note the staggering implication that Common Sense can tell us what God has in mind for us and for the world—all that we need to know.

Nothing is more significant in Jesus' parables than his appeal to Common Sense. What a pity that this term has been abused to mean no more than sweet reasonableness or, worse, public opinion. Rightly understood, it means the deep awareness that all have in common and from which anything sensible must flow. We could even say that Common Sense is God's Holy Spirit in the human heart. And here Jesus differs from the prophets. They appealed to the authority of God as standing behind them—"Thus speaks the Lord God. . . ." Jesus, in contrast, appeals to Common Sense, to the authority of God in the hearts of his hearers.

No wonder the people felt empowered. "This man speaks with authority," they said, and they added, "not like the Scribes" (Mark 1:22), not like the authorities of cultural religion. This comparison triggered the earthquake of an authority crisis from which the world is still shaking; it also sealed the fate of Jesus and made the disastrous end of his career practically inevitable. In our own time, experience teaches that one has to pay a high price for standing up for God's peace and justice in the face of authoritarian law and order.

As the very opposite to conventional thinking, Common Sense was, and still is, subversive to authoritarian structures and intolerable to their religious as well as political representatives. Appeal to Common Sense can have dangerous consequences; for Jesus, the final consequence was his crucifixion.

Why make such a point of this?

The statement that Jesus was CRUCIFIED, in the context of the Creed, means more than recording a point for the historical record. The Creed is all about proclaiming one's ultimate trust in God. But to affirm that faith in God when faced with the crucifixion of Jesus (and all the innocent suffering in the world symbolized in his cross) is a pledge of allegiance to the vision for which he lived and died—the Kingdom of God, a world order built not on might but on love—on the Yes to belonging without borders of any kind and with all the consequences entailed by this Yes.

Faith in Jesus CRUCIFIED means putting one's ultimate trust in God's Kingdom, in spite of the fact that he and innumerable others who followed him died for this vision without seeing it realized. But did they? Could it be that their very striving unto death to realize this vision of Jesus was its realization in this world? Perhaps we may be permitted to paraphrase A. J. Muste's saying, "There is no way to peace—peace is the way." There is no way to God's Kingdom— God's Kingdom is the way. Or, as Saint Catherine of Siena put it: "All the way to Heaven is Heaven"—even the way of the cross. To glimpse this truth, to experience it just a little, for instance when we enjoy the pain we suffer for the sake of someone we love, makes it possible to have faith in God not only *in spite* of Jesus' crucifixion, but *because* of it. Jesus CRUCIFIED modeled an altogether paradoxical way of realizing God's Kingdom in and by his death.

This faith does not presuppose any particular interpretation of Jesus' death, no why or wherefore. But the human mind wants to know why Jesus had to die on a cross and what this means for us. The mind needs interpretations for everything it perceives, all the more so for an event so challenging to faith. Not all, however, who recite the Creed must hold the same interpretation. The most important aspect of CRUCIFIED in the Apostles' Creed is the absence of any interpretation (in contrast to the "for our sins" in the Nicene Creed). This point can never be sufficiently stressed. This early Creed is truly catholic; it does not define and exclude like the later ones. On the contrary, it makes room for all who do not exclude themselves by insisting on definitions and interpretations. This Creed breathes freedom; it summarizes the essentials of faith in God and leaves the rest wide open. Many will find this liberating. By stating faith in Jesus CRUCIFIED without providing an interpretation, the Creed faces us with the challenge to find our own.

There is room for ever-new interpretations. Every period in history must find its own. Not all proposed interpretations of CRUCIFIED over the course of the centuries are helpful today. Some of them prove outright harmful to spiritual health. Unfortunately this is true for the most widely disseminated and most thoroughly misunderstood interpretation, which insists that Jesus died *for our sins*.

This interpretation has become for many Christians an insurmountable hurdle to faith. "What kind of God," they ask," would demand the cruel death of his son?" Certainly not the God of the Christian Good News. Therefore the meaning of Jesus CRUCIFIED deserves a closer examination here.

Forgiveness of sins is already an integral aspect of the earliest accounts of Jesus' crucifixion for theological as well as historical reasons. It is helpful to begin with the historical ones.

Forgiveness of sins plays a crucial role in the life of Jesus and ultimately brings about his death. Jesus awakened and strengthened in his followers the faith that God had forgiven their sins, and this without reference to the Temple authorities in Jerusalem, who had a "divine" monopoly on releasing people from the social as well as psychological burden of sin. Forgiveness of sins was legally regulated. It was dispensed and supervised in detail by the priestly caste. But Jesus bypasses this system and assures repentant sinners with full confidence of God's forgiving love: "Your sins have been forgiven" (e.g., Luke 5:23, 7:48). This was dangerous. It brought him into conflict with the official priestly sin-and-forgiveness system. His interference in this delicate matter made him liable to be accused of blasphemy, for which the penalty was death (by stoning; it took the closely related political charge of sedition to bring about Jesus' crucifixion). Thus, forgiveness of sins does not begin with the death of Jesus, but is rather the very core of his healing and teaching throughout his life and becomes a major reason for his execution.

So much for the historical connection between Jesus' death and forgiveness of sins. The theological connection goes back to a key question that the earliest Christian community had to face: How could God permit the death of Jesus?

As they searched their sacred scriptures for an answer, passages in the biblical book of the prophet Isaiah provided the decisive clue. Speaking of a mysterious "Servant of the Lord," the so-called Servant Songs in Deutero-Isaiah contain passages that could readily be applied to Jesus, and offered an answer. The decisive words read, "Surely he has borne our grief and carried our sorrows; yet we esteemed him stricken, smitten by God, and afflicted. But he was wounded for our transgressions; he was crushed for our iniquities; upon him was the chastisement that brought us peace, and with his stripes we are healed" (Isaiah 53:4f).

Obviously referring to the Isaiah passage just quoted, Saint Paul wrote to the Christians in Corinth, barely more than two decades after the crucifixion: "I delivered to you as of first importance what I also received: that Christ died for our sins in accordance with the Scriptures" (1 Corinthians 15:3). Isaiah's scriptural interpretation gave meaning to the cruel death of Jesus and was of prime importance to his followers, and has been so to Christians ever since.

Yet, in the two millennia since, this interpretation was elaborated into an ever more legalistic notion of substitutionary suffering, the belief that a vengeful God demanded that Jesus earn the world its salvation by accepting a brutal punishment on behalf of humanity in exchange for their sinfulness. Today this represents a massive relapse into the very mode of thinking that Jesus vigorously opposed by preaching an all-forgiving God. He was CRUCIFIED, and paid for this with his life. But now, ironically, his death is interpreted as presupposing a vengeful god.

So prevalent is the notion of Jesus' substitutionary suffering that many Christians forget it is no more than an interpretation, and, in its final consequences, is incompatible with Jesus' own image of God as loving Father. We need to free ourselves of the legalistic mentality perpetuating wrong and harmful interpretations. We also need to recover early Christian ways of thinking about the death of Jesus on the cross. Such scriptural interpretations of CRUCIFIED are helpful to us today. Only three shall be mentioned here.

1. Jesus was CRUCIFIED to make peace

Under the perspective of this New Testament interpretation, the cross of Jesus becomes an ensign of peace. The arms of the cross connect left and right, above and below. It is the compass rose, the cosmic cross that marks the coordinates of the universe. Many ancient spiritual traditions know and venerate this figure of the cross. It is usually depicted with vertical and horizontal arms of equal length. Saint Paul seems to have this image in mind when he prays for his fellow Christians to be able "to grasp how wide and long and high and deep is the love of Christ, and to know this love that surpasses knowledge" (Ephesians 3:18f).

Jesus strove all his life to help people find peace—within themselves, among one another, and with God. He lived for peace. And since his life and his death are of one piece, he also died for peace. With his last breath he prayed, "Father, forgive them, for they do not know what they are doing" (Luke 23:34). Thus his cross becomes the plus sign joining together, shortly after his resurrection, the most diverse people in one and the same community. "For God was pleased to have all his fullness dwell in him, and through him to reconcile to himself all things, whether things on earth or things in heaven, by making peace through his blood, shed on the cross" (Colossians 1:19f).

2. Jesus was CRUCIFIED to overcome death

In the light of the resurrection the early Church saw Jesus Christ elevated on the cross as triumphant and victorious. He is Life, and life has conquered death. "Death has been swallowed up in victory. Where, O death, is your victory? Where, O death, is your sting? . . . Thanks be to God! He gives us the victory through our Lord Jesus Christ" (1 Corinthians 15:54–57). For the first thousand years of Church history, Christian art translated the CRUCIFIED of the Creed into a bejeweled cross, and later into Christ on the cross as crowned victor.

3. Jesus was CRUCIFIED to blaze a trail for us
into true joy

This interpretation finds its expression in a third New Testament model for understanding the crucifixion: "Jesus, the pioneer and perfecter of our faith, who for the joy set before him endured the cross" (Hebrews 12:2). Jesus is here called "pioneer," because, trusting in God, he forged on ahead of us into unknown territory. Everything within him recoiled from death, and from so horrible a death. "Then he said to them, 'My soul is overwhelmed with sorrow to the point of death. Stay here and keep watch with me'" (Matthew 26:38). "And being in anguish, he prayed more earnestly, and his sweat was like drops of blood falling to the ground" (Luke 22:44). And yet he remained faithful to his path of nonviolent revolution and bore the consequences. Walking ahead of us in faith all the way into the darkness, he became not only the pioneer but the perfecter of faith for all who follow him. Passing through death, he becomes the "pioneer of life" (Acts 3:15). This perspective is diametrically opposed to vicarious suffering. One aspect is particularly appealing: it takes the anguished searching of Jesus seriously, and so encourages us to have patience in our own.

Every period in history has to find its own interpretation of the CRUCIFIED in the Creed—always in light of the resurrection. (Helpful books on this subject are, among others, *Jesus through the Centuries*, by Jaroslav Pelican and *Meeting Jesus Again for the First Time*, by Marcus Borg.) What is important, however, is not the interpreting of suffering but our effort to relieve the suffering of others and to bear our own with faith in God's love. On this path, which Jesus pioneered by word and action and which in Buddhism is the Bodhisattva path, we may hope to find the joy of meaning in suffering which cannot be put into words.

Personal reflections

As I grew up, I often heard references to one or the other relative or friend of my family who was said to have "a heavy cross to bear." This notion of following Jesus by bearing one's own cross sprang up in the earliest Christian community and found its expression in the Gospels, where Jesus is quoted as saying to those who want to become his disciples, "Take up your cross and follow me." Under Roman rule, following in Jesus' footsteps may indeed have led to crucifixion, but for countless other Christians throughout the centuries, the cross they bore with courage, patience, and love had nothing to do with the reasons for which Jesus was crucified. In what sense, then, can I, in the twenty-first century, speak of bearing my cross, when this means, say, suffering the disadvantage of being honest, caring for aging parents, or dealing with a debilitating sickness? What is the connection between my "cross" and that of Jesus? The key connection is faithfulness. Jesus did what faithfulness to God demanded in his life story, and I am to do the same, no matter how different my own life story may be.

Jesus wanted his cross no more than I want mine. The cross we choose is no real cross. But we choose to be faithful to God, no matter what it costs us, and "cross" symbolizes that cost. On the

Mount of Olives, Jesus himself prayed for an easier solution: "Father, if it is possible . . ." But he struggled through to "Your will be done." Making that same phrase their own when they pray the Lord's Prayer, Christians of every walk of life have overcome resentment against their lot, and so found the "peace that passes all understanding" (Philippians 4:7). You will recognize such a peace by the deep inner joy that is quite compatible with pain. Physical as well as emotional pain can be embraced by a serene joy that arises as soon as we drop resentment and accept what is. This is not resignation, but its very opposite. Only non-resentment makes a creative response possible—and often an unexpectedly creative one.

As long as I can remember, my mother had this saying in a small frame on her desk: "These are the strong ones in the land: They laugh among tears, hide their own pain, and give joy to others." In German it rhymed, so I remember this maxim well. But I remember it all the more vividly because my mother lived it. Those who live it are not weighed down by their cross, but rather lifted up, raised beyond their own suffering to a firm footing from which they can help others find peace. Pain, it has been said, is inevitable in life, but suffering is optional. Bearing one's cross in patient love is the traditional Christian way of overcoming suffering.

Born and raised a Catholic, the mythologist Joseph Campbell (1904–1987) was an outspoken critic of the overemphasis on suffering that used to be so widespread among Christians. As a scholar of sacred images, he recognized a masochistic attitude expressed in many crucifixes. Shortly before his death, he underwent treatment in a Catholic hospital. His widow, Jean Erdman, told me about a different kind of crucifix found in his hospital room, a contemporary representation in which a triumphant Christ stands with raised arms on the cross. When Joseph Campbell saw this, he exclaimed, "This is the crucifix I was hoping to see all my life."

———

And you? What image of Christ CRUCIFIED, if any, appeals to you? (Remember that for the first half of its history the Christian tradition knew no image of the crucified, only a bejeweled cosmic cross—a cross with four arms of equal length, a compass rose for the spiritual journey.) Have you been taught interpretations of Jesus' death on the cross that made you question God's love? How have you dealt with them? Are you familiar with people who, inspired by Jesus Christ CRUCIFIED, took upon themselves heroic suffering for the sake of others (for example, Saint Maximilian Kolbe, who volunteered to take the place of a fellow prisoner in a concentration camp and died an excruciating death)? Have you ever experienced the joy of overcoming suffering by bearing pain for the sake of others?

Died and Was Buried

~

What does this really mean?

The affirmation that Jesus DIED relates back to BORN in an earlier section of the Creed and emphasizes that we are dealing here with the full human reality from birth to death. To the eyes of faith, the immediate reality of our whole life span between birth and death becomes a receptive vessel for the presence of God. Like Jesus, we must learn to put our faith in God, amid the pleasures and pains of daily living, and not get lost in the abstractions of philosophical or theological speculation.

DIED AND WAS BURIED also means gone, a failure—radically wiped out by the domination system opposing him, and to which he was opposed. This marks the negative pole to which the resurrection will provide the positive counterpole.

As a historical corollary—not as a statement of faith—BURIED also implies that the corpse of Jesus was identified and handled by witnesses and put in a grave. This seems to have been highly unusual for victims of crucifixion, yet all four Gospels tell us in detail about the burial of Jesus. Our understanding of the Resurrection will depend on our evaluation of the historicity of these accounts.

How do we know this is so?

Historical facts must be established by research. Beliefs based on faith are no valid substitute for this historical verification process. At present, this process is in full swing, scholarly opinions are divided, and the question, "Was Jesus buried?" is being hotly debated.

On the basis of first-century burial statistics, some scholars say no. (Hardly any buried remains of the tens of thousands of crucifixion victims have been found.) On the basis of sindology—the study of funeral shrouds—other scholars say yes. (The so-called Shroud of Turin, bearing the imprint of a crucified corpse, has strong historical and forensic claims to being the burial cloth of Jesus. These claims are strengthened by the Sudarium of Oviedo, the cloth that covered the head of the corpse depicted on the Shroud; blood type and location of head wounds agree, and the history of this relic is better known.) Historical certainty will have to await further research. Faith, in contrast, refers to an indisputable fact: Jesus was eradicated by his opponents. This sets the scene for the Creed's "and yet" of the resurrection.

Why make such a point of this?

In view of the resurrection of Jesus, it is of great importance to affirm DIED AND WAS BURIED, its counterpoint. Both dying and being buried belong to the full humanity of Jesus. Dying is our ultimate activity; in contrast to being killed, the verb *dying* does not even have a passive voice. Being buried, on the other hand, helpless like a thing, signifies ultimate passivity. Both can become transparent and transformed by God's love shining through. In this light I realize that my own dying and ultimate helplessness belong to that unique word of God which is my life. It comforts me and gives me courage to know God is always close to me, in death as in life. DIED AND WAS BURIED in the Creed reminds me of this and gives form to my confidence.

Personal reflections

Death and burial are woven into the very fabric of our lives, from the deaths of our childhood pets and the funerals children stage for birds they find dead by the bushes to the great bereavements of adult life—one's child, a spouse, or an intimate friend. When I came back for the first time after twenty years to the place where my brothers and I had buried our pet canary, the two tiny saplings we had planted on the grave had grown into tall trees—one tall tree, in fact, for the two tree trunks had been placed so close together they had merged into one.

It was my privilege to be present at the deaths of my mother, my grandmother, and my great-grandmother. My mother had said, "This is how I'd like to die. I'd want you to sit where you are sitting now holding my hand, and I'll just fall asleep." Three days later she did just that. My grandmother died while Mother and I were praying the rosary at her bedside. And her mother died one evening when she and I, then six years old, were alone at home, and she had just read a story to me.

Close as I was to my mother and her mother and her mother's mother when they died, I was disconnected from my father's death in a surprising way. Knowing he was preparing to die, my brother and I had flown to Austria from the United States, had had a warm and cheerful visit with him, and said our final goodbyes. Two weeks later I was lecturing in Hawaii when I received a telephone call informing me of my father's death on June 21. Where I was in Hawaii, it was still June 20. A few hours later I boarded a plane for Austria, where I arrived on June 22. So June 21, the day of my father's death, never occurred among the days of my life.

In contrast, what a comfort to gather with family and friends for a wake at which those who stay behind can support one another as they share memories of the one who went before them. I experienced this among the Tohono O'odham in the Sonoran Desert, where a dead man was propped up in a sitting position, and all who came in shook hands with him and talked about unfinished business before taking leave of him. My Maori friends in Aotearoa (New Zealand) invited me to a *tangi*, the funeral ritual at which the body of the deceased is never left alone between death and burial, but is surrounded by relatives and friends who come and go, while the body lies in state on the *morae* (the ceremonial ground), sometimes for days. It is not uncommon for a wedding to take place on the same *morae* at the same time, and I found it refreshing to be with a people whose culture has a vivid and deep awareness that death and life are of one piece like the curled shoots of the *ponga* ferns pushing up from decaying tree trunks in the forest.

What are your own memories of death and burial? Can you live with them long enough, look at them lovingly enough, to see them as ripples in a ceaselessly flowing stream? And further, can you see the flow of divine Life itself reflected in these events?

He Descended into Hell

❧

What does this really mean?

After a series of historical statements we are once again confronted with a mythical reference. The image of HELL was familiar to Jewish tradition as Sheol and to the Greeks as Hades—the realm of death, the abode of the dead. A more accurate translation of the Latin *descendit ad infernos*, would be "he descended into the realm of death."

Like the emphasis on the "three days" in the next statement of the Creed and the "died and was buried" in the previous one, HE DESCENDED INTO HELL wants to stress that Jesus was truly dead, not just apparently so. In addition, the emphasis falls on Jesus' sharing the common lot of mortals. He became one of the countless multitudes who died before him, especially those who were killed as victims of injustice. Jesus' death—and therefore also his resurrection—is neither an isolated event nor a private affair. (We will find this equally affirmed in regard to the resurrection of Jesus.)

This solidarity of "God's beloved Son" with all of God's children even in the realm of death finds further elaboration in the first letter of Peter, chapter 3, where Jesus is portrayed as proclaiming the life-giving power of the Spirit "to the spirits in prison," to those who had gone before him into Sheol (1 Peter 3:19). To the first generation of Jewish Christians this myth expressed a necessary consequence of the death of Jesus Christ: the prison bars of the netherworld could not hold the one who was Life personified. He would burst open Sheol's gates and so liberate all the other inmates as well. This finds a vivid pictorial expression in the icons of "Christ's harrowing of hell."

If we ask what it meant for the dead that Christ DESCENDED INTO HELL, we are mistaking a poetic image for a historical account. But the justified concern behind this question might be expressed in this way: What does it mean for our understanding of death that Jesus Christ and countless other innocent victims before and after him had to die? To this question, DESCENDED INTO HELL does imply an answer. Basically it simply affirms that he was really dead, but this cannot be separated from the deep trust that the Psalmist expresses in the words, "You will not abandon me to the grave, nor will you let your Holy One see decay" (Psalm 16:10). Death is not a prison, but a passageway. Since this is true also of the many deaths we have to die throughout a lifetime, faith that Christ DESCENDED INTO HELL—every conceivable hell—can bring to human hearts deep consolation.

How do we know this is so?

HE DESCENDED INTO HELL does not refer to an action of Jesus. It is not on the same level as statements like "he got into a boat," or "he descended from the mountain." Regarding those two statements it is reasonable to ask, "How do you know?" and the answer will ultimately have to be based on observation. But if we could ask the Christians who put HE DESCENDED INTO HELL into the Creed, "How do you know this is so?" a likely answer would be, "Well, I told you already. He died."

Since the descent into hell is simply a poetic way of saying that Jesus died, we might want to ask a different and more appropriate question: Why use this mythic image and not another? Why use mythic imagery at all? The answer is that this was the common myth of those who cast the content of their faith into the form of this Creed, a content too rich to be enunciated in more brittle language than that of poetry. Do we then have to make this myth our own if we want to recite the Creed with integrity? No, not the imagery of this myth, only the truth it wants to express: No realm of human experience in life and death, not even HELL, is beyond the reach of God's love, a love powerful enough to set us free.

Why make such a point of this?

HE DESCENDED INTO HELL is a helpful reminder of God's presence in every realm of existence. Nothing can separate us from the love of God, even in the most hellish regions of our inner world. This thought is also a fitting preparation for the communal aspect of the next phrase in the Creed. If the one who represents God's love shared the common lot of all who died, they in turn will have a share in the triumph of that love—in his resurrection.

Personal reflections

Jesus of Montreal (1989) is still my favorite among the Jesus films that flashed across the screen in recent decades. Director and writer Denys Arcand links the story of Jesus with concerns of our own time, and the Jesus whom Lothaire Bluteau portrays vibrates with a passion and compassion I find convincing. The story Arcand tells is clear-cut: A group of actors is hired by a church in Montreal to present a passion play. Their unconventional interpretation delights the audience but enrages church authorities. Daniel, who plays the part of Jesus, inspires his fellow actors to go through with the project and begins to mirror in his own life the life of Jesus: his passion (in the sense of zest, dedication, and intense effort to stage the play against all efforts of those who oppose him) becomes his Passion (in the sense of suffering and death).

Arcand's script shows both depth and humor in finding contemporary parallels to the Gospel account. Daniel's selecting actors for the play reflects Jesus' calling his disciples; when an enterprising lawyer takes him to a restaurant overlooking the city and offers him an enticing commercial career, we are reminded of the tempter's "all this will I give to you"; as Jesus stood before Pontius Pilate, Daniel stands before a wavering judge in court. The scriptwriter set himself an almost insurmountable task, however, when he decided to present also Christ's descent into hell, yet he met this challenge admirably. The beaten and wounded Daniel, left neglected on a stretcher in the emergency room, gets up and, in his delirium, staggers down into a subway station to visit the homeless encamped there in the bowels of the city.

We have hell, the netherworld, and the realm of the dead closer at hand than we may like to remember. And what is the point of believing that Christ descended into that region if we are not willing to do so with him? In the Creed, we profess our faith that God's loving presence can be found there, too. Who then shall be God's ambassadors? A dear and admired friend of mine, a person of international renown, sends me every year her Lenten resolutions for prayer, fasting, and almsgiving. One year she wrote, "I will give some money to the homeless in our streets, but I will also give each one a hug."

And you? In which "realms of the dead" can you become an ambassador of God's love? Befriending the homeless is only one of countless other ways to do so. Is there a retirement home in your neighborhood where old people feel lonely and abandoned? What visit or telephone call could be, for you, a descent into hell and, for the one you called, a ray of sunlight breaking into the dark?

The Third Day He Rose
Again from the Dead

What does this really mean?

The most basic meaning of this clause is that even though Jesus was dead, dead, dead (for "three days"), he now lives. He was only a guest, as it were, in the realm of death. In many cultures, guest privileges are limited to three days. Even in the monastery, guests who stay longer than three days are expected to help with the chores. THE THIRD DAY HE ROSE AGAIN FROM THE DEAD proclaims triumphantly: Even though Jesus was condemned, and executed by both the religious and the political authorities, God vindicated him by giving him indestructible life and ultimate authority.

This clause of the Creed proclaims Jesus Christ to be a living force in the world, vindicated and empowered by God, though he was annihilated by the powerful of this world. In the world order we know, there is no place for peace and justice, for equal distribution of material and cultural goods, and for the dignity of every human being. Jesus took a stance for those values and was cynically disposed of as a rabble-rouser. The worst part was that for a Jew of Jesus' time, condemnation by the religious authorities meant unquestionable condemnation by God. Jesus pioneered the unthinkable conviction that even in this respect God's ways are not our ways. That God did not prevent his death seemed to prove him wrong and settle that point. Yet, by "raising him up," God vindicated all that Jesus stood for. This is what counts here. An empty tomb, a risen body, and apparitions to his followers are helpful illustrations for some people, obstacles for others. The Creed sticks to essentials: God vindicated the one whom the world condemned to death; behold, he lives.

HE ROSE is not the earliest form of the Easter proclamation. The original "God raised him up," focuses more clearly on vindication and is logically more correct. Because being dead implies ultimate powerlessness, the genuinely dead Jesus can rise only if he is first raised. This is seen in one of the earliest Christian texts—Saint Paul's first letter to the Thessalonians. There we find both forms side by side. In chapter 1, Paul refers to the faith of the Christians at Thessalonica in Jesus whom God "raised from the dead" (1 Thessalonians 1:10). In chapter 4 he writes, "We believe that Jesus died and rose again" (1 Thessalonians 4:14). In fact, Paul stresses here the communal implications by adding, "and so we believe that God will bring with Jesus those who have died with him." Both formulations express faith in God as giver of life and vindicator of justice, and this is what we mean when we say, THE THIRD DAY HE ROSE AGAIN FROM THE DEAD.

How do we know this is so?

What kind of proof can we expect for the resurrection? Suppose Jesus walked up the steps of the Vatican one day, or into a 12-step meeting (where he'd feel more at home)—would this constitute proof that HE ROSE AGAIN FROM THE DEAD? If you think so, you have the wrong notion of resurrection. It has nothing to do with coming back to life (like Lazarus in John's Gospel). The Creed does not talk about any coming back; resurrection is a movement forward and upward unto a new level of life.

To know what Jesus stood up for means seeing his life as a manifestation of divine wisdom, compassion, and power. But this wisdom is foolishness in the eyes of the authorities who wiped him out; this power is weakness. And yet "the foolishness of God is wiser than human wisdom, and the weakness of God is stronger than human strength" (1 Corinthians 1:25). We are dealing here with the wisdom and power of love, and "love is as strong as death" (Song of Solomon 8:6). The Bible knows this, and human beings know it in their heart of hearts. On THE THIRD DAY—signifying a sacred moment of completion and new beginning—the power of love must break the bonds of death. Love's full manifestation cannot be suppressed forever, even by death. Christians expressed this certainty by putting into the mouth of Jesus a passage from the prophet Hosea, which they translated as, "I will be your death O death!" (Hosea 13:14).

The followers of Jesus experienced the resurrection of Jesus Christ as a life-changing conviction. Boldly they could now live by the ideals Jesus had lived by, and they could say to their religious authorities, "We must obey God, not men. The God of our fathers raised Jesus from death, after you had killed him by nailing him to a cross" (Acts 5:29f). This boldness was based essentially on an inner experience, verifiable by their enthusiasm. But was there an outward trigger for that experience and that enthusiasm? This is a valid question, and the answer can be subjected to historical verification. Historians demonstrate a wide variety of opinions on this point, selecting on the basis of prior convictions even what data they will take into consideration. On one end of the spectrum are those who see some historical basis in the Gospel accounts, and, on the other, those who discredit those texts altogether. We have a right to demand all relevant material available at this time to be taken into account. This includes textual analysis and archaeology, as well as artifacts like the Shroud of Turin and the Sudarium of Oviedo, which exegetes are only beginning to take seriously. So it is still an open question what was the outward trigger for the disciples' faith that THE THIRD DAY HE ROSE AGAIN FROM THE DEAD. For those who pray the Creed, it is faith in the vindication of Jesus by God that matters. This faith will make all the difference for the way they live: as Jesus lived, empowered by the Spirit that empowered Jesus.

Why make such a point of this?

Faith in God is what the Creed is all about. This cannot be said too often. Belief that God's beloved Witness was not abandoned—not even when he cried out, "My God, my God, why have you forsaken me?" (Mark 15:33), not even in the realm of death—speaks above all about God. It presupposes a distinctive view of God. It makes the point that God is concerned with justice and does set things right, though not necessarily on the level of history. At all times, and especially in our time, this is certainly a point worth making.

In the midst of a world whose politics, economics, and dealings with the environment are death-bound, faith in Jesus' resurrection gives us power to live God-determined lives, and enthusiasm to realize God's plan for the world, "that they may have life, and have it to the full" (John 11:11). We may want to know more about what we can and should do based on the resurrection. Concretely, how does faith in God's vindication of Jesus change our way of thinking? How does it connect us to our true selves? How does it increase our faithfulness? How does it shape our actions? An exemplary life story may be the best answer to these questions, and the towering example of Dag Hammarskjöld offers itself.

This Swedish diplomat was born in 1905, became the second secretary general of the United Nations in 1953, and was killed in an air crash during a peace mission in 1961. John F. Kennedy admitted, "In comparison to him, I am a small man. He was the greatest statesman of our century." Only after his death was this man of action revealed to the world as a true mystic when his notes and diaries were posthumously published under the title *Markings*. The theologian Henry P. Van Dusen called this book "perhaps the greatest testament of personal faith written . . . in the heat of professional life and amidst the most exacting responsibilities for world peace and order." In his foreword to *Markings*, the English poet W. H. Auden quotes Hammarskjöld as stating, "In our age, the road to holiness necessarily passes through the world of action." Dag

Hammarskjöld was placed in one of the highest positions the domination system had to offer. Inspired by Jesus, he used the power this gave him to empower others for peacemaking and economic justice. Like Jesus, he could foresee what this would mean for his own career. With foresight he wrote, "We are not permitted to choose the frame of our destiny. But what we put into it is ours. He who wills adventure will experience it—according to the measure of his courage. He who wills sacrifice will be sacrificed—according to the measure of his purity of heart."

"For all that has been—Thanks. For all that shall be—Yes," is Dag Hammarskjöld's best-known quote. But we have to read his *Markings* to realize the depth of soul-searching from which this Yes sprang. "I don't know Who—or what—put the question, I don't know when it was put. I don't even remember answering. But at some moment I did answer *Yes* to Someone—or Something—and from that hour I was certain that existence is meaningful and that, therefore, my life, in self-surrender, had a goal." In the Second Letter to the Corinthians, Saint Paul calls Jesus "the Yes of God" (2 Corinthians 1:19). Once Hammarskjöld had found that Yes, he wrote, "As I continued along the Way, I learned, step by step, word by word, that behind every saying in the Gospels stands *one* man and one *man*'s experience. Also behind the prayer that the cup might pass from him and his promise to drink it. Also behind each of the words from the Cross."

Dag Hammarskjöld knew, "He who has surrendered himself to it knows that the Way ends on the Cross." That cross came for him in 1961. The fifty-six-year-old secretary general of the UN was en route to negotiate a cease-fire on the night of September 17–18 when his airliner crashed near Ndola, Northern Rhodesia (now Zambia). The circumstances remain unexplained, but former president Harry Truman is reported to have said, "Dag Hammarskjöld was on the point of getting something done when they killed him. Notice that I said 'when they killed him' "—just like Jesus when he was on the point of getting something done. Jesus called that something God's Kingdom. All who share Hammarskjöld's faith in the risen Christ will, at the point of death, be able to say with him, "I was certain that existence is meaningful and that, therefore, my life, in self-surrender, had a goal."

Personal reflections

The essential message of Christ's Resurrection is that the life, work, and message of Jesus, although rejected by the authorities who executed him, were approved by God, and God thus vindicated Jesus, the crucified outcast. But how did this happen? What took place on that Easter morning—historically? Although faith in the living Jesus validated by God's authority is all that ultimately matters, the question remains: On what is this faith based? If my faith is based ultimately on the faith of the Apostles as the first witnesses, on what was their faith based? A question like this does not, it seems to me, spring from mere curiosity.

It does not suffice to prejudice our search for an answer by either accepting the Gospel accounts uncritically or rejecting their witness due to some preconceived conviction. True, they are not historical accounts, according to our modern understanding of historicity. But they relate data that can be considered likely or unlikely, possible or impossible, by our contemporary historical standards. For a long time I have been interested in two such data mentioned in the Gospels: the empty tomb and the burial cloth.

It is true the Resurrection accounts differ far more widely from one another than the Gospel accounts of Jesus' life, but all four of them have the same starting point: the empty tomb. They claim unanimously that Jesus' body disappeared miraculously from the place where he lay buried, and then Jesus appeared to his disciples afterward for a limited period of time. With regard to the form these appearances took, the Gospel writers go their separate ways. Anthropology was my minor when I studied at the University of Vienna for my Ph.D. in psychology. So I asked myself as an anthropologist: Do we find any similar accounts in other cultures? (I mean reports about supposedly historical events similar to the resurrection stories in the Gospels.) This would give us points of comparison and allow us to check whether such things actually happen. We must not assume that something is a unique event in history before checking whether maybe it has happened elsewhere. And remember, we are here concerned with supposedly historic events on Easter morning, which is quite different from faith in the Resurrection. Serious Christians today believe in Christ's resurrection without taking the Easter stories as historical accounts. But then we are back at the question, was there no historic trigger to Resurrection faith?

I vaguely remembered reports about Tibetan teachers whose corpses supposedly shrank dramatically in size or disappeared altogether, and I promised myself to follow this up someday. Well, as it goes with questions like this, I procrastinated for years, but one nice morning I decided, today I am going to start checking this out! I sent a fax to my friend Vanja Palmers, a Zen teacher in Switzerland, and urged him to ask around among the many Tibetans who had found a new homeland in the Swiss Alps. Within days I got a reply. To Vanja's surprise, a Tibetan teacher had come to visit him. Vanja told him of my question. And to his even greater surprise, the visitor told him of a teacher of his in Tibet who had just died and disappeared in this way two or three months earlier.

Now or never, I thought. Someone has to go to Tibet to check this out. My friend Monsignor Francis Tiso immediately came to mind, and I contacted him. He had written his doctoral dissertation at Columbia University on the Tibetan sage and saint Milarepa, and had visited Tibet. Was he planning another trip there? Yes, he was—in three days! Would he be able to sidetrack to Switzerland for a quick briefing? Against all odds, he was able to fit this into his plans, and so started a long research project on the Rainbow Body phenomenon, later funded by IONS (the Institute for Noetic Sciences), a project that continues to this day.

What I learned was that the Rainbow Body phenomenon is well documented in texts going back for centuries, and it is still occurring today. It is as well attested as any anthropological phe-nomenon. Typically, a teacher will request, prior to his death, that his body be left undisturbed for a specified time—say, a week or two—and during this time the body, covered with a cloth, will shrink or disappear altogether, at times leaving behind hair or fin-gernails. What I found particularly significant is this: In addition to this empty-tomb syndrome, the teacher who died will appear to his disciples (and—like Jesus—to his disciples only, not to the public) for a limited period of time. We have here phenomena highly rem-iniscent of the Resurrection accounts in the Gospels—events that take place in our own time so that we can check them out—and scholarly integrity obliges us to do so for the purpose of potential verification or disproval. Thus it seems imperative for exegetes of the Gospel accounts of the Resurrection to familiarize themselves with these facts, as they are available now. But will they do so?

This question brings me to the burial cloth of Jesus. For a cen-tury now, the Shroud of Turin has been the object of extensive sci-entific investigation. Yet exegetes have almost completely ignored these findings. The Shroud is a strip of linen fourteen feet long by three and a half feet wide, in herringbone weave familiar to ar-chaeologists from Egyptian mummy wrappings. It bears the faint, full-length body imprint—front and back—of a corpse that was en-folded in it at burial. Experts in forensic medicine have examined every detail of this relic and concluded that the man on the shroud had been scourged, nailed to a cross, and pierced through the heart with a lance, in precise agreement with the details in the Gospel ac-count of Jesus' last hours. What scientific studies were unable to as-certain was how the image on the Shroud was created. What we see there actually resembles a photographic negative. No paint or other media used by artists were found on the Shroud. All known means of creating an image have been eliminated.

A carbon-14 radioactive dating test in 1988 was widely dis-cussed in the media and seemed to indicate that the Shroud was only some seven hundred years old. Since then, however, it has been established that the sample tested was not part of the original cloth. The Shroud's antiquity has also been challenged for lack of documentary attestation before 1360. However, Ian Wilson, in his book *The Blood on the Shroud*, presented a well-documented hypothesis for the history of the Shroud before that date, and pollen analysis confirmed that Wilson had correctly traced its traveling route back from France to Constantinople, Edessa, and Jerusalem. Pollen specific to these places was found embedded between the linen's fibers.

A still more convincing confirmation of the Shroud of Turin's age comes from comparing it with a different relic, the so-called Sudarium of Oviedo in Spain, which has been venerated there since the eighth century as the cloth with which the blood was wiped from Jesus' face. Its history is well documented and leads back to Jerusalem, a travel path confirmed by pollen analysis in this case, too. All four Evangelists mention that Jesus was wrapped in a linen cloth for burial, and John's Resurrection account mentions this cloth again in the empty tomb together with a "cloth that was over Jesus' head" and lay there "separate," "not with the other clothes," "in a place by itself." The Sudarium of Oviedo may well be this cloth, for its blood type (AB) and bloodstains perfectly match those on the head seen on the Shroud of Turin.

Of course we will never find any "proof" that the man whose blood is on the Shroud and on the Sudarium was Jesus. Yet what we know today gives me an indication of what triggered (not caused!) the original witnesses' faith in Christ's resurrection, namely an empty tomb and an image on a shroud. After all, this is what John's Gospel succinctly says about the disciple whom Jesus loved best: "He saw all this"—the burial clothes in the empty tomb—"and he believed" (John 20:8).

And you? What do you consider a possible trigger for the disciples' faith in the Resurrection after their disastrous disappointment on Good Friday? Is there something in on THE THIRD DAY HE ROSE

AGAIN that helps you in your dark hours? Do you know people who are empowered by the Resurrection to swim, as Jesus did, against the current of the world's ways? (They don't have to be as well known as Dag Hammarskjöld. It is enough "to do the common things of life in an uncommon way," as George Washington Carver said.) What is most uncommon, as you see it, about the stance Jesus took in the world? Does the Resurrection give you an incentive to take a similar stance?

He Ascended into Heaven

What does this really mean?

Like DESCENDED INTO HELL, ASCENDED INTO HEAVEN does not mean Jesus Christ *did* something. Rather, just as DESCENDED is the mythopoetic elaboration of the statement HE DIED, so ASCENDED elaborates the statement that God raised him up: HE ROSE. In the centuries during which the Creed was formulated, the myth-making power of the human mind flowed more abundantly than in our own desiccated and disenchanted time. The dramatic imagery of levitation into the clouds before heavenly and earthly witnesses, in Luke's Gospel and Acts, bears witness to a fertile imagination delighting in vivid visualization of a firm conviction: Jesus Christ is risen and is with God.

If we want to know what it meant to the first Christians that Christ ascended INTO HEAVEN, we must consult scholars of ancient languages. Linguistic analysis of first-century Aramaic, Hebrew, and Greek usage has established that, in the New Testament, "Heaven is not a place or a state." However, so ingrained is this notion of a Paradise in the sky—whether or not we believe that it exists—that it costs us an effort to imagine a different meaning of the term *Heaven*. So, what did it really mean? Scholars do not make things easy for us when they say that *Heaven* was understood as "a dynamic point of departure" from which God's power breaks into the world. This does not feed our imagination the way a heaven in the clouds does. But if we think of Jesus Christ as "sent by God" in the sense of being an ambassador of God's love, he is "heaven-sent" in a sense in which the English language approaches the original meaning of *Heaven*. The risen Christ returns then to his point of departure; he ascends—to use a different metaphor—to the source from which God's love gushes forth. This is, of course, the epitome of bliss, and this bliss aspect covers also the more familiar notion of Heaven, as perfect and illimitable joy.

What, then, does this clause add to the proclamation of the resurrection? HE ROSE proclaims that he is alive; HE ASCENDED INTO HEAVEN wants to say with what kind of life he is alive: with God's life. In the biblical worldview, HEAVEN is also the firmament, the blue sky, and as such it is thought to conceal the abode of God, who is "enthroned above the heavens" (Psalms 11:4; 103:19). In this mythopoetic imagery God is concealed by the firmament. We cannot see God, but we can experience the divine blessing as life-force throbbing in the veins of the universe. The risen Christ is with God. Thus, like God, the risen Christ is concealed, hidden. Yet his power to move human hearts—to compassion, to self-esteem, to deep respect for others—continues to be at work in the world. His life is "hidden . . . in God" (Colossians 3:3); this is the central meaning of this passage in the Creed.

How do we know this is so?

We experience divine life as "hidden." It is the life within all aliveness, hidden as the spring is hidden in the stream. We can sense the current of this hidden life as it guides all things from within, pulsating as blessing—the cosmic bloodstream—through the universe and through our own innermost being. Even a passing awareness of this life within us gives us the assurance that its power is not subject to decay. All forms arise and vanish, but what makes sense to the human heart is the intuition that what Dylan Thomas called "the force that through the green fuse drives the flower" is itself indestructible and will eventually return to its hidden Source.

Almost as if commenting on a Christian's personal inner experience of the passage HE ASCENDED INTO HEAVEN, the early Christian martyr Ignatius of Antioch wrote in the year 107 to the community in Rome, "Living and speaking water is within me, saying deep inside me, 'Home to the Father.' " Those who dare to flow with this stream will sense its direction.

Why make such a point of this?

All this would not be important as a "Hooray!" for Jesus Christ, who ascended to the top of all possible ladders. It is important, however, as a statement about our own innermost life, the Christ-life, a life seemingly so powerless by worldly standards, one might doubt its existence entirely. Here we proclaim our true life as "hidden with Christ in God" (Colossians 3:3)—"hidden" also in the sense of "hidden away" for safekeeping—in God, whose power is hidden in weakness, yet "stronger than human strength" (1 Corinthians 1:25). Understood in this sense, HE ASCENDED INTO HEAVEN is empowering for all human beings, regardless of their particular religious tradition.

In all three Gospel accounts of the Ascension and in the Acts of the Apostles, different as they are in other respects, Jesus commands his disciples to go into the world and teach. Although this commission to bear witness to the Kingdom of God is not explicitly mentioned in the Creed, this Mission Statement, as we may call it, resonates clearly as an overtone in HE ASCENDED INTO HEAVEN. Those who proclaim this passage of the Creed with full faith take it upon themselves to faithfully carry out the mandate, "Go into all the world and preach the good news to all creation" (Mark 16:15). If the risen Christ is "hidden in God," it is only through the compassion, labor, and creativity of those who have faith in him that he can work in the world.

A passage like the one just quoted shows the cosmic implications of the Good News. Of course this is a mandate to preach not so much by words but by deeds. The risen Christ is hidden in God, and God is hidden in the cosmos—in every smallest particle of it. The task to proclaim this "to all creation," to all creatures, implies responsible stewardship of our environment. HE ASCENDED INTO

HEAVEN implicitly makes this point, and those whose lives reflect the faith proclaimed in the Creed will have to make it explicitly.

Personal reflections

Whenever you are trying to find a gift for a friend, consider giving a poem—one that touched you when you came across it, or maybe even one that you wrote yourself. It would be hard to find a more personal gift. Some of the poems that have come to be lifelong companions for me were gifts from friends. The poet Patricia Campbell Carlson, known to people all over the world through her remarkable work on the website www.gratefulness.org, once brought me a poem which I like to reread every year on the Feast of Christ's Ascension. Ascension Day comes at a lovely time of the Church's liturgical year, forty days after Easter. This is springtime in our woods around Mount Saviour Monastery, and trillium is in bloom—"white as Christ's robes when He ascended into heaven."

With an easy touch, the poet takes this large white flower— one only on each sturdy stalk that rises from the ground—and sets it side by side with Christ rising toward heaven in white garments. Skillfully she weaves a third image into the poem: heaven, as the sky drawn with a child's blue crayons. Small children draw the heaven above houses and trees as a blue line across the top of their pictures. Only at a later stage of development do they fill in the background of their landscapes with blue sky. Subtly this hints at a fuller understanding of Christ's ascension.

When I was a child, this was what I heard when the account of Christ's ascension was read or preached about: Forty days after his Resurrection—the same length of time as the forty days of Lent in preparation for Easter—Christ takes his disciples to the Mount of Olives, where his Passion began, and there he is lifted up before their eyes, rising into the sky, until a bright cloud hides him from view. Two angels are suddenly standing there and tell his startled disciples that he will come again—as judge of the world on the last day, we took this to mean, although the angels didn't say this.

Today, when I read the same opening passage of the Acts of the Apostles, it is as if a searchlight were pointing to passages and key words of that text to which I never paid attention before. *Witness* is such a key word. Christ's last words tell his followers that they will be his witnesses. This turns our eyes from gazing to the sky and makes us face the task before us. In the power of the Holy Spirit the Apostles—and we—will carry the Good News to the very ends of the earth. This makes me think of a brave community of witnesses, Benedictine women, almost two thousand years later and literally "at the end of the earth," viewed from Galilee. They arrived in the mid-nineteenth century in what were then the wilds of Minnesota. There they and their successors bore witness by teaching many hundreds of thousands of Minnesota schoolchildren not only the "three Rs," but also the joy of beauty, truth, and goodness. Today they have taken up another timely and equally important task of witnessing: they are struggling to prevent a superfluous highway project and to preserve forestland white with pristine stands of trillium. (It takes these rare flowers five years from seed to bloom.)

On the wide map of ways to witness "to all creation" have you found your personal way?

A spotlight shines also on another passage when I read it these days. While formerly I thought that Christ was leaving when he ascended to heaven, I read his rising and his being hidden by a cloud differently now. The bright cloud—as in the accounts of Jesus' baptism and his transfiguration—symbolizes God's Presence. So, Christ is "hidden in God." And as God's Presence fills the universe, so does Christ's. This is the "place" he went to prepare for us. This is where I hope to be, with him and in him, when this death-bound form, called by my name, is no longer around.

I now read Christ's being "lifted up" as image language echoing a passage in the letter to the Ephesians that speaks of God putting all things "under his feet" (Ephesians 1:22). As a beautiful paraphrase puts it: God has put everything without exception into Christ's power, and God appointed Christ as head of God's household. The community is Christ's body, and God fills the universe with the whole fullness of Christ's vitality. Thus, when I kneel down on the moist forest floor to look a trillium straight in the face, I see in it also Christ's body, pulsating with aliveness.

I see it, and I see it not. Thus, light falls on another passage I had never noticed until my dear friend and revered teacher, Ramon Panikkar, opened my eyes for it. Christ will come again, the angels tell his disciples, "just as you saw him go." I used to think: up he went; down he will come. But no. He will come "in the same manner in which you saw him go"—raised up (to a different level of being) and hidden (in God).

A child learns to color the whole sky, as the poem below states, and I learned to see that the heaven into which Christ ascended is all around me. He becomes visible for me in the face of the trillium, but just at that moment the cloud of God's invisible presence hides him. It is always in going away that he is coming. It is in just *having* seen him that I see him. Do you? How *do* you personally experience the risen Christ? Is his presence-in-absence more readily accessible to you in nature or in other human beings? In what way do you see your hands and feet and ears and eyes as potentially the risen Christ's hands, feet, ears, and eyes?

Trillium

> All along this hill: trillium
> white as Christ's robes when
> He ascended into heaven,
> rinsing the breeze free of impediment
> on slender stems that stretch below
> the moss into the rich, dark dirt.
> What was His stem when
> He went to prepare a place for us?
> Heaven used to be a strip across

the top of my crayoned page,
with never any stairs to get there.
All at once, the bottom drops out.
The trillium draws light from millions
of miles away and streams it down
to even the most secluded root.
A child learns to color the whole
sky.

—PATRICIA CAMPBELL CARLSON

He Sits at the Right Hand of God the Father Almighty

~

What does this really mean?

This is another poetic image in the series of statements that unfold and spell out the implications of Christ's resurrection. Vindication (HE ROSE) and exaltation (HE ASCENDED) culminate here in empowerment (AT THE RIGHT HAND OF GOD). Sitting enthroned, Christ is here depicted as wielding ultimate power—which can only mean the power of love, the only ultimate power there is. Name your favorite saint—a witness to heroic love in any of the world's traditions—and you will have named an example for wielding the power of love. It is, of course, in weakness that the saints wield power. "When I am weak, then I am strong," said Saint Paul (2 Corinthians 12:10). Saint Francis and Mirabai, both ecstatic singers of divine love; Ramakrishna and Catherine of Siena, mystics on different continents in different centuries; Florence Nightingale and Mary McKillop, helpers of the helpless: they all were poor and weak, and yet they wielded world-changing power. C. S. Lewis spoke of this power as "the union of a kneeling with a sceptered love." As "God's right-hand person" Jesus holds a position of highest authority. The proclamation of Christ's authority in this clause of the Creed points forward to the next, which will spell out the actualization of that authority: TO JUDGE.

To someone who cannot appreciate poetic and mythic imagery, these passages in the Creed will mean nothing. One needs to acquire this sensitivity, not only to be able to understand the Creed, but to have a full appreciation of the better part of life—from

Shakespeare's plays to Rumi's poems, and from the *Bhagavad Gita* to any love letter that will ever be written. All children have the eyes, ears, and hearts of poets. All they need is a minimum of encouragement—someone who looks when they see a bug and shout "Look!," someone who listens with them to the many different sounds of water, or to the sounds of wind. We need to give children time to really get to know a tree, smell it, touch it, climb it, learn its name rather than just call it "a tree." We need to give them plenty of time to daydream. Later, when we fall in love, we get another chance to let our heart speak its native language: poetry. Romantic love finds itself tongue-tied until it finds its own words of poetry. This would be the time for language teachers to introduce teenaged students to great love poems and to encourage them to write their own. Is it by chance that so many drop out of Sunday school at precisely the same age at which they lose interest in poems? Only people with a healthy sense for poetry will be able to appreciate what a majority of passages in the Creed really mean.

How do we know this is so?

This clause contains no new "information"; it does not add to what we already know. It merely draws out one more implication of faith in Jesus Christ as alive and active. We know that the fate of Jesus is repeated again and again in history. It is the fate of all who strive to live with integrity by the guidance of their inner light and stand up for justice. The authoritarians whose pseudo-authority counts in this world will strive to annihilate them. They annihilated Martin Luther King Jr., who comes to mind as one example among countless others. But even though he would not live to see the fulfillment of his dream, he knew that "the arc of history is long but it bends towards justice." Authentic authority that uses its power to empower others will win in the end by convincing people. Our deep authentic Self resonates with this conviction. Thus we know that God will vindicate all witnesses to justice, as God vindicated Jesus Christ who SITS AT THE RIGHT HAND OF GOD THE FATHER ALMIGHTY.

The title LORD, which we gave to Jesus Christ early on in the Creed, implies all this. And reference to THE FATHER ALMIGHTY implies that the kind of power and authority of which the Creed speaks is not that of an autocratic potentate, but of a caring father. Love is all-powerful because one who suffers appalling injustice, affliction, and even death lovingly can give them meaning. And meaning is ultimately all that matters. Thus we know in our heart of hearts that the authority of love with which Jesus taught and acted remains valid even beyond time. No suffering can make void the authority of love. And the Creed proclaims this authority.

Why make such a point of this?

The vindication series of statements in the Creed (ROSE, AS-CENDED, SITS enthroned, SHALL COME TO JUDGE) turns step by step more directly from Jesus Christ toward *us*, hammering out the importance of his resurrection, by drawing out ever more clearly the implications for every human heart.

By proclaiming Jesus Christ as invested with divine authority, we acknowledge this authority as resonant with the authority of our own authentic selves. And by thus acknowledging what Jesus Christ stands for as being authoritative for us, we in turn take our stand with him—for peace, justice, nonviolence, and compassion. We stand with him as we comfort the sick, feed the hungry, embrace the unloved, and replace indifference with caring.

The genuine dignity of every single human being is solemnly promulgated when we affirm that Jesus Christ—representing the quintessential human—SITS AT THE RIGHT HAND OF GOD.

Personal reflections

It was a highlight of my journey through northern Italy to look up into the apse of the cathedral of San Vitale in Ravenna. A youthful, beardless Christ is seated—not on a throne, but on the cosmos itself, depicted as a sphere of radiant blue afloat on the background gold that represents divine mystery. With his left hand he holds a book propped up on his knee; his right arm is extended to hand a crown of victory to Saint Vitalis. He is flanked by two angels, the one on the right putting his hand on the shoulder of Saint Vitalis, the other reaching out to the bishop who built this church and carries a model of it on his arm. Christ's whole figure seems to vibrate with vitality. His neck is that of an athlete. His huge dark eyes under their high-arched brows are the eyes of a poet. His head is surrounded by a delicate halo that combines a circle with a cosmic cross. His feet are firmly planted on the ground where flowers bloom and the four rivers of Paradise gush forth. But as the eye moves upward, Christ's body seems to float upward, too, toward rosy clouds suspended in the gold of heaven.

As I stood there wide-eyed, sheer beauty sent shivers down my spine. But something moved me still more deeply: my awareness to stand before a monument to human dignity, to the ultimate dignity of even the despised, the discarded, the forgotten. Pascal knew it, and the image of Christ enthroned depicted it before my eyes— that the human infinitely surpasses the (merely) human: *"L'homme dépasse infiniment l'homme."*

Jesus Christ enthroned—an image towering above the altar and filling the apse of a basilica with golden glory. After almost fifteen centuries we see this mosaic in all the freshness of its original splendor. When the scaffolding came down and those who crowded into this church could for the first time see these mosaics, the average life span of the men and women who stood there wide-eyed was perhaps thirty years. And those few years were filled with hardships unimaginable for the tourists who stand today where they stood then. How must it have felt to the unwashed and underprivileged throughout the centuries when they entered these churches, to see a human form—their own—raised to such glory?

The same realization was thrust at me in a most unlikely situation. It was at a low point in my life when I saw the surpassing glory of the human shine from the faces of two dozen men who transformed a crowded, smelly barracks room into holy ground. Advancing German troops had "liberated" the village in Russia that the ancestors of these men had established as a tiny island of German culture centuries ago, and these young men still spoke a form of German that had been spoken then. Their wives and little children were now in a refugee camp, and they, like me, had been forced into the German army.

Don't ask me why I ended up in their platoon as the only one not from their village. The only reason I can see, as I think back on it, is this: I was to witness the glory of God—human beings fully alive—in the midst of the daily grind of boot camp. It was all so ordinary, yet I am still reeling, a lifetime later, from the culture shock I experienced. These were genuine human beings at their best, even under such dismal conditions. They laughed with light hearts, in spite of it all. They dared to weep, and they had plenty of reason for that. They joked a lot, but I never heard one dirty word— and this in a barracks, remember. I still remember how they talked from bunk to bunk after lights-out about their families, heartbreakingly. They showed one another (and me) the spontaneous kindness and caring one might expect from a platoon of monks— fine monks.

On the very day that basic training ended, they were shipped to the front lines. Why was I left behind? I never knew. Their train, because of some crossed wires at headquarters, took them straight into a station Russian troops had occupied. Legally they were Russian citizens and therefore traitors. No news ever came back. But when I see the image of Christ in glory, through his eyes the eyes of every one of these men look at me.

When and where have *you* found yourself eye-to-eye with indestructible human dignity? And if you think that this never happened to you, what do you think it would be like if it did happen? Do you see what faith in Christ, the archetypal human, humiliated by the powers but exalted by God to the position of highest power, might do for the oppressed and exploited in the world today? Does it make sense to you that poetry can be the language of nonviolent revolution? And do you see this power of poetry in a phrase like HE SITS AT THE RIGHT HAND OF GOD THE FATHER ALMIGHTY?

Thence He Shall Come to Judge the Living and the Dead

What does this really mean?

The opening word THENCE refers back to the previous clause of the Creed and indicates that the power TO JUDGE is a further aspect of the vindication, exaltation, and empowerment that the Resurrection implies. We have a verbal mirror image here. Three clauses unfold what it means that Jesus Christ ROSE. They correspond to three clauses indicating what CRUCIFIED implies. Three negative images lead down to DESCENDED, and this corresponds to ASCENDED, with which the three positive images for his rising begin. The one who descended into hell now ascends into heaven. The one who was buried in the place of ultimate weakness, the grave, now sits enthroned in the place of ultimate power, "at God's right hand." The one who died, killed by injustice, now comes as judge to make justice the dividing line between the dead and the truly living.

In these mirror images the Creed displays a word pattern of great beauty.

To ferret out what is meant by TO JUDGE THE LIVING AND THE DEAD, we must dig like archaeologists through more-recent layers of interpretation in search of earlier, more-basic ones. The top layer consists of a widespread misunderstanding that springs from taking poetry literally—a problem we have encountered before. Words of Jesus about divine judgment that their Gospel context shows to belong to a literary form called "apocalyptic" are taken as predictions of future history. The Greek word *apokalypsis* means "the lifting of a veil," a "revelation" of God's saving will. When Jesus speaks about a new order, brought about by God's will, to judge the domination system and to vindicate the oppressed, he uses poetic images of cataclysmic world events. This is typical for the apocalyptic style of his period, as for example in the Book of Revelation (also called Apocalypse). But a later mentality takes these images no longer as revealing God's will through metaphor but as revealing the future. Now the "Second Coming" is seen as an event at the end of time, when Jesus Christ shall come "again," this time as judge. Michelangelo depicted this view overpoweringly. A more primitive layer of interpretation does not historicize the reversal of fortunes, but simply takes it to mean his enemies judged him, but now he will judge his enemies. On the next deeper level we find the underlying intuition in its raw form: "All wrongdoing will eventually find retribution." On the deepest level this insight springs from the existential awareness that justice cannot be permanently repressed. In our peak experiences, for instance, we may convincingly intuit this aspect of reality, in spite of all the injustice we see daily around us. Maslow's psychological research showed that many subjects whom he questioned about their peak experiences bore witness to the deep insight that justice is simply a basic quality of being (a B-value, in Maslow's terms).

Depending on our understanding of TO JUDGE, the meaning of THE LIVING AND THE DEAD will differ. On the surface level it means those still alive at the Second Coming and those who died before. On the deepest level it means that only those whose lives are attuned to divine justice are truly alive; the others are more dead than living. Justice is a matter of life and death since it is an aspect of our very being.

Rightly understood, Jesus Christ does not judge by doing, but simply by being—not by being the judge, but by being the judgment. A well-built chair judges in this way sloppy craftsmanship, Dag Hammarskjöld judges politicians, Cesar Chavez judges union organizers, and any exemplary human being, say, Dorothy Day, judges our whole society. In this sense, the supreme standard of spiritual aliveness set by Jesus Christ is a judgment not only on the cold indifference of the spiritually DEAD, but also on the halfheartedness of those who, in T. S. Eliot's apt phrase, "have gone on living. LIVING and partly living."

And this is good news. For we must distinguish justice from revenge. Judging does not mean punishing, but setting things right. Genuine justice "justifies" in the way a printer justifies the lines on a page by making the margins straight. In the Creed, judging means reestablishing divine wisdom and compassion as the principle of a new world order. The very laws of the old order, under which we live, spring from hate, greed, and delusion, and perpetuate injustice. "Exploitative normalcy," is what J. D. Crossan calls this state of terminal social dysfunction. In contrast, a just world order springs from love in action.

How do we know this is so?

If the statement HE SHALL COME TO JUDGE THE LIVING AND THE DEAD refers to a future event that it is believed will happen, no one can know whether it is true or false. We'll have to wait and see. If, however, it refers to the place of justice in the scheme of things, experience allows us to evaluate its claims. Justice is not a matter of imposing laws, as one imposes, with a cookie cutter, patterns on flattened dough; more like the yeast in the dough, it makes things work from within.

Justice puts reality in sync with being. We know this in our peak moments, when we drop preconceived notions and come face-to-face with reality. We know justice intuitively and on a much deeper level than notions of right and wrong that have been drilled into us, or that we willingly made our own. Even when we act unjustly, we know justice. Even our rage against what appears to us as God's *in*justice springs from an ineradicable conviction that fair play ought to win in the end.

Why make such a point of this?

When we find in this phrase of the Creed, underneath the mythical imagery, its practical implications, we realize how helpful it can be for putting our life in order. Wherever genuine order unfolds—say, in the drip-by-drip growth of an icicle, in the development of a cherry pit into a tree, or of two lovers into a family—this process follows a law, not imposed from without, but inherent in it, and the law within all laws is wisdom and love. Order is never static; it is a dynamic unfolding, ever-changing, like the images in a kaleidoscope.

In nature, whatever we look at closely shows itself "justified"—in harmony with divine order. If we understand love as "the full Yes to belonging," nature is the great example of love in this sense: all of nature is a great celebration of the mutual belonging of all to all. Only we humans introduce the rift of alienation into the seamless fabric of natural order. Yet our hearts do intuit the plumb line of God's justice, and Jesus Christ makes it explicit. The Harvard psychologist Lawrence Kohlberg (1927–1987) mapped the stages of moral development during a person's lifetime. He holds that justice is the central characteristic of moral reasoning. The heart seeks to right itself according to justice, the way a compass needle rights itself according to magnetic north. Kohlberg agrees with the wisdom of great moral leaders like Gandhi, Cesar Chavez, or Martin Luther King: the principle of justice requires that we respect the basic dignity of all human beings. Justice applies to all, and is therefore universal. In actual practice, Kohlberg says, we can reach just decisions by looking at a situation through the eyes of others. Note how this attitude of deep empathy exemplifies "the Yes to belonging." It is a Yes to what the Vietnamese Buddhist monk and teacher Thich Nhat Hanh calls "Interbeing." Justice is rooted not in law but in love. Yet no matter how obvious the general guidelines of wisdom and love may be, the process of orienting ourselves accordingly is made exceedingly difficult by the complexity of life's circumstances. Just think of political, economic, and environmental decisions—and in some way everyone is a "decision-maker."

Jesus lived and died for justice (for which "righteousness" is merely the Sunday-going-to-church term). Crystals, lichens, ants, leopards, and Jesus—each in their own way and on their own level—give us examples of justice by the way they live their great Yes to belonging; thereby they also "judge" us and the way we live. Our decision to live as best we can by God's justice is the border crossing from the realm of the DEAD to the land of the LIVING.

This land-of-the-living theme constitutes the segue to the next and final portion of the Creed, which will be devoted to the Holy Spirit, the spark and flare and blaze of full aliveness on all levels.

Personal reflections

From where did we get our nightmarish imagery of Christ's "Second Coming"? How did Michelangelo conceive the idea, depicted in his Last Judgment in the Sistine Chapel, that the Madonna would have to pull her veil tightly around her head and shoulders and turn her eyes away from the violent gesture of her son, the World-Judge? Yes, I do admit to feeling anger toward some criminal heads of state and their economic advisers, and I, too, might sometimes wish for such a judge. In my better moments, however, I know that God's patience can achieve more by "a lingering-out sweet skill," as Gerard Manley Hopkins puts it, than with any destructive lightning bolts and thunder clashes of judgment. Thus I make the poet's prayer my own, emphasizing the "rather, rather."

> With an anvil-ding
> And with fire in him forge thy will
> Or rather, rather then, stealing as Spring
> Through him, melt him but master him still

My favorite lines about Christ's "Second Coming" are in the story "A Christmas Memory" by Truman Capote. In this autobiographical piece of great delicacy, the author describes his last Christmas with the woman who brought him up. The author is seven at the time, she is in her sixties, a childlike soul radiant with inner beauty. They are each other's best friends. On Christmas Day, the two of them are lying in the grass, flying the kites they made as presents for each other. Suddenly the old woman experiences a moment of mystic insight. She admits that formerly she had imagined Christ at the Second Coming shining like the windows in a Baptist church, sunlight pouring through the colored glass. But now she realizes with utter surprise and delight that what she has always seen—what we always see all around us—is Christ in glory, here and now.

Could it be that Christ's real "Second Coming" will be just such an eye-opener, and thus be a judgment on our failing to see that he had been coming all along? Do you have memories of moments that helped you "right" your life according to the plumb line of an inherent divine order? Did you experience those moments like a thunder crash or rather like a gentle thaw in spring? How do you resonate with this saying by the Spanish mystic poet Saint John of the Cross: "At the end of life, we shall be judged *by love*"?

I Believe in the Holy Spirit

What does this really mean?

The repetition of the solemn I BELIEVE indicates that another part of the Creed begins here, the third and last one. It does not point to a third something in which we believe. There is only one target toward which ultimate faith shoots the different statements of the Creed like so many burning arrows: the Ultimately Actual (also known, in the Creed's less fancy language, as God). We experience our relationship to this singular reference point of existential trust in three different ways:

1. We find our innermost Self open for God as the ultimate horizon.
2. We keep discovering God as the unfolding mystery we are to ourselves.
3. We breathe with every breath God as our very life, the Holy Spirit.

This explains why there are three parts to the Creed.

SPIRIT signifies life-breath, aliveness—the breath within our every breath. We can become aware of our limited life as a participation in a limitless aliveness experienced as pure gift: THE HOLY SPIRIT. In biblical language, the opposite pole to SPIRIT is "flesh"— meat that no longer breathes. Flesh stands for everything that is bound to physical decay or rottenness and frustration on any level of existence. The polarity of flesh and spirit must never be confused with the complementary relationship of body and mind.

The divine SPIRIT is called HOLY in the sense of awe-inspiring and fascinating. Wherever the life-force erupts naked and with irresistible power, it both lures us and strikes us with dread. This double aspect of the sacred characterizes any awareness of THE HOLY SPIRIT.

How do we know this is so?

We can become aware that living is not something we *do*, like jogging or cooking, but rather a process in which we participate by whatever we do or suffer. This process is at the same time within us and beyond us. We can understand it not by intellectual analysis, but only by experience. We can distinguish levels or degrees of that aliveness. Your favorite meal will raise your aliveness to a certain level; your favorite piece of music will raise it a notch higher; holding your firstborn in your arms will mark still another level. And you may even find yourself in a situation in which your sense of physical aliveness is lowered by illness or old age, emotionally you feel low, even your mental aliveness seems diminished, and yet precisely in such moments you may become aware of a deep inner intensity, a flame of life, steady and strong in spite of your flagging vitality. We tend to pay no attention to that innermost flame of our aliveness as long as our overall vitality is more robust. When it enlivens our longing for the Ultimate and empowers us to serve others, Christians call this aliveness-within-our-aliveness HOLY SPIRIT. Any human being can experience this transcendent life-force, regardless of the name one gives it.

Why make such a point of this?

The point of I BELIEVE IN THE HOLY SPIRIT is not to assert the opinion that there is "a divine Person called Holy Spirit." Rather, those who proclaim this sentence in the Creed express thereby their deep trust in life—in the life pulsating through our bodies and animating our very being, the life we share with all that is alive, the life that is ultimately our participation in divine aliveness. To trust life means having faith that the flow of life will always bring us what we need, though not always what we want. If we really trust in life, we will not waste our energy on resentment, on wishing that our life's circumstances were different from what they are; rather, we will use all our energy for responding appropriately to the given situation—to bloom where we are planted.

People who have faith in life are like swimmers who entrust themselves to a rushing river. They neither abandon themselves to its current nor try to resist it. Rather, they adjust their every movement to the watercourse, use it with purpose and skill, and enjoy the adventure.

What could be more decisive for our outlook on life and our attitude toward it than this basic trust? The more we wake up to the mystery of life, the more we become overwhelmed by the inestimable gift it is to be alive. To realize this makes us ever more grateful, with every heartbeat, with every breath. This grateful living, in turn, leads to ever-increasing joy in life.

The next sections of the Creed draw out, step by step, what is already implied by I BELIEVE IN THE HOLY SPIRIT. In contrast to theological speculations about the inner life of God, our Creed presupposes no more than we can deduce from full awareness of our own inner life. This must be the focus also of our study here.

Personal reflections

In the late 1960s, Ann Arbor, Michigan, was known as "the landing strip of the Holy Spirit." John XXIII, "Good Pope John," as the whole world called him with affection and admiration, had prayed for "a new outpouring of the Holy Spirit," but he himself could not have anticipated how overwhelmingly his prayer would be answered. Starting with a veritable explosion of spiritual gifts during a students' retreat at Duquesne University in February 1967, the Charismatic Movement erupted in the Catholic Church and spread with lightning speed to all parts of the globe. Suddenly ecstatic "praying in tongues," prophetic utterance, and the gift of healing, long familiar to Pentecostal churches, were now practiced in any mainstream parish. Not long before, I remember asking in a theology class why these gifts, so conspicuous in the early Church, were no longer in evidence. My professor assured me that these extraordinary manifestations of the Holy Spirit were no longer needed; Church institutions had replaced them. Well, it was to the credit of the institutional Church that it—cautiously but firmly—supported this grassroots spiritual renewal. Under the leadership of Ralph Martin and Stephen Clark, the Word of God Community in Ann Arbor became the spiritual center of this movement.

This was also the time of the House of Prayer Movement, a rediscovery by active religious communities of their contemplative core, and I had been invited to help set up more than a dozen such houses for temporary monastic life in Michigan. As might be expected, there developed a lively exchange between the two movements. Many went regularly from their silent houses of prayer to the bubbling charismatic prayer meetings. Many of us prepared for Baptism in the Holy Spirit, a renewal of one's baptismal commitment combined with a special openness to the power of God's spiritual gifts. For myself, I had chosen July 20 for that ceremony, because that day was the forty-third anniversary of my baptism. Little did I anticipate what added significance that date would receive in 1969. As we came out of the prayer room, aglow with enthusiasm, the first thing I saw was the full moon high in a tall window. A small crowd had gathered there in the hall, in front of a television set. They stood in awestruck silence, watching live as the first human being set foot on the surface of the moon. "That's one small step for a man, one giant leap for mankind," we heard Neil Armstrong say.

The timing could not have been better for me; it was perfect. To this day I can hardly believe how well everything fit together to hammer home for me a lasting insight: Yes, the Holy Spirit stirs our hearts to religious fervor, but the passionate and patient research of scientists, the creativity of artists, musicians, and writers, and the ingenuity of men and women dedicated to the service of others in a thousand fields of human endeavor all spring from the same Holy Spirit.

Each string of a wind harp responds with a different note to the same breeze. What activity makes you personally resonate most strongly, most deeply, with the wind of the Spirit that blows where it wills? The excitement of the Charismatic Movement in the sixties and seventies has subsided, but the mainstream churches will never be the same. Countless Christians learned to test doctrine by experience; they will never go back to subjecting personal experience uncritically to official doctrine. How do you assess independent thinking in religious matters? Does it have limits that ought to be respected? How would you see the role of the HOLY SPIRIT in this respect? In your experience, where is the Spirit moving in the world today?

The Holy Catholic Church

⟿

What does this really mean?

This phrase of the Creed draws out an implication of the previous one: Faith in the Spirit implies faith in the CHURCH. But why? And what does CHURCH mean? Living is always an interaction with countless other living beings—a community of plants, animals, humans, and the unseen higher forces at work in the world. Just to recognize this is an important step; but to put one's trust in this connectedness and act as one acts toward those with whom one belongs together is the decisive step. Since life is precisely what we share with a community that includes all living beings, it can never be a private affair. What one does affects all. And faith in the Spirit, Source of all Life, means faith in community. THE HOLY CATHOLIC CHURCH is that community.

The Holy Spirit creates HOLY community. "All those who are led by the Spirit of God are sons and daughters of God" (Romans 8:14). This means that all who live in harmony with the divine dynamics at work in nature and in history constitute the community called CHURCH. It is for those people we must look—both inside and outside the institutional churches—if we want to find the HOLY CHURCH. This phrase of the Creed does not assert that a particular institution called "church" is holy—that it manifests divine life. Rather it is the other way around: wherever divine life manifests itself in community we are in the presence of CHURCH, the *Ecclesia*, the community of those who follow the call of the Spirit.

The all-pervading Spirit that "fills the whole universe and speaks every language," as the Christian community sings on the

Feast of Pentecost, the Spirit who "holds all things together" (Wisdom of Solomon 1:17), creates the all-embracing, that is, CATHOLIC, community. Rightly understood, CATHOLIC (Greek *katholicos* or "all-embracing") is not a copyrighted label for a particular sector of Christianity (an "all-embracing sector" is an oxymoron to begin with). Rather, men and women anywhere in the world and at any period of history who served others out of a sense of universal belonging show us what it means to belong to the one community that deserves to be called CATHOLIC CHURCH.

The earliest definition of CATHOLIC faith that the Christian tradition developed is still valid and valuable today. Seen in a new light and understood in our contemporary context, this definition, proposed by Vincent of Lérins around 450 CE, can be helpful in a new way. Vincent described the CATHOLIC faith as a faith that has been held "by all, at all times, in all places." In his time, "all" meant all Christians. But our horizon has grown wider. For us, "all" means all human beings. There is no longer room for a narrower understanding of catholicity. Truly CATHOLIC is only that faith in Life and its ultimate Source that all humans share. It remains alive in the hearts of humans who are not even aware of it. It can be awakened by any religious tradition.

Catholic faith is not a specific brand of Christian faith, but Christian faith is one particular form of catholic—i.e., universal—faith. The CATHOLIC CHURCH in which one can have faith is the community of *all* who have faith, to whichever of the world's religions they belong. It is understandable that many Christian communities today replace the word CATHOLIC in the Creed with "Christian" in reaction to the Roman Church's calling only itself CATHOLIC—an *ex*clusiveness that contradicts the *in*clusiveness of that term. It would be more faithful to the spirit of the Creed, however, to translate the word CATHOLIC as "all-embracing" rather than replace it with a narrower term, even the term "Christian."

The Creed wants to exhibit, point by point, what faith in God implies. One of these implications is CHURCH, a living community inspired by the living God. In the realm of history, any such community needs an institutional framework. But one can have faith in the full sense only in God, never in an institution.

Any particular Christian community can realize only a fragment of the CATHOLIC whole. As a member of that Christian community whose institution calls itself "Catholic," I am deeply grateful to my Church for the innumerable gifts I have received from it. The greatest gift, however, is this: within the framework of my Church, I have been given glimpses of THE CHURCH. It is this CHURCH in which I profess my faith when I recite the Creed—the truly HOLY CATHOLIC CHURCH, a community that bursts every framework.

How do we know this is so?

We start with Spirit as an experiential reality. We realize that life, and thus life in the Spirit, is always life in community. A community giving expression to the Spirit—through full, genuine aliveness—will have the marks of the Spirit. It will be HOLY—mediating an encounter with the divine, and manifesting the life-creating energy of Spirit, in opposition to the self-destructive forces of fear, violence, and oppression. And it will be CATHOLIC—an all-embracing community of universal sharing and caring, in opposition to greed, exploitation, and prejudice. Christians call this community CHURCH, meaning originally "the Lord's house." "Now the Lord is the Spirit," as Saint Paul writes, "and where the Spirit of the Lord is, there is freedom" (2 Corinthians 3:17). You will know genuine CHURCH community by the freedom it lets you experience, both by the support it provides and the choices it leaves open.

It would be difficult to come to this understanding if we started with any given institutional church and went on to prove that it is HOLY and CATHOLIC. Few would be convinced. We may hope and trust, however, that many members of every institutional church belong also to CHURCH as community in the Holy Spirit. At their best, churches can become windows through which we can glimpse, and gateways through which we can enter, CHURCH.

Why make such a point of this?

Our lives are shaped by the communities to which we belong. There are communities whose members are bonded by fear or vanity; they pride themselves on exclusivity, anger, or conspicuous consumption. Can you think of one close to home? Michael Moore has exposed some of them, setting box-office records with his documentaries. There are also communities bonded by mutual trust and compassionate service; their members support one another's courage, creativity, and generosity. When local churches are at their best, they become examples of this kind of community. Thus there are consequences in stating clearly to what kind of community we want to belong. And when it comes to putting our radical trust—the faith we put in God—in a community that is HOLY and CATHOLIC because it is alive with God's very life, our choice has radical consequences.

In spite of their institutional shortcomings and crimes, communities of all religious traditions keep witnessing to the power of love in the world, through the shining example of their finest members. Dissatisfaction with religious institutions, as they are, springs from a longing in the human heart for what they could and should be. Your criticism of your Church may or may not be inspired by the Holy Spirit. It will prove justified if you go beyond criticizing and *do* something to make THE HOLY CATHOLIC CHURCH a reality in your own Church. The world longs for this manifestation of life-giving community.

Personal reflections

In a public Buddhist/Christian dialogue, Zentatsu Richard Baker Roshi once asked me to assume for a moment that my Christian faith was simply wrong—just to clear the ground for an unbiased exchange between the two of us. His request seemed reasonable to me, and I agreed. Closing my eyes, I tried to wipe my inner slate clean of all Christian convictions and commitments. The harder I tried, my eyes still tightly shut, the more impossible this task became. Finally I laughed out loud, "I simply can't do it." Since then, I have sometimes asked myself, *why* not? Why could I not make this simple thought experiment? Because a great deal more than thought is involved. And this is where the Church comes in.

My Christian faith is not an opinion I could suspend for the sake of argument. Rather, it is the ground in which my life has its roots—I can express it only in images—a foundation much deeper than thought. My faith is embedded in my experience of a community in whose embrace I grew up and to which I belong as to a family, and that is the Church.

At Baptism, the candidate has to ask the formal question "What do you ask of the Church?" and the one-word answer is "Faith." This does not mean a list of teachings printed in a book. It means the living witness of courageous human beings that only a community can give. Dorothy Day and the Catholic Worker Communities, or Cesar Chavez and the United Farm Workers, are witnesses to a Christian faith that became a force for social change. So is Dr. Martin Luther King Jr.—and here "my Church" expands beyond the confines of my denomination. With Mahatma Gandhi— to stay with the same line of witnesses—my Church expands even beyond Christianity. The more lovingly we are rooted in the family of our birth, the more readily will we acknowledge our membership in the all-embracing human family and live accordingly. We will feel secure and thus less prone to the fear that fosters exclusivity. In much the same way, being at home in a particular Church can help us expand our sense of belonging until we see the whole world as God's Household.

My Church is for me a symbol of that God Household—a symbol in the full sense: a sign embodying that surpassing reality to which it points. We do need symbols as anchors in reality. My young friend, standing next to me in a papal audience, was surprised when he saw me kiss the Pope's ring. This ring, too, is a symbol within that symbol which is the CHURCH.

The great witnesses I mentioned earlier stand out in my mind when I think of the Church, but they are the bright shining lights. There are also hidden ones who, in their own way, forged my understanding of CHURCH no less powerfully. There was the witness of our parish chaplain in the final days of World War II, Father Geiger Alois. (He always put his family name before his given name, as the Austrian peasants used to do, with whom he identified.) There was no water, no electric power, our neighborhood was a field of ruins, and the ragweed that grew from the rubble was our staple food. No one knew what the next day would bring, but this faithful priest would make his rounds through the devastation, and at 5:00 P.M. we covered a chest with a clean cloth and lit a candle, for we could count on it that he would bring us Holy Communion. On that morning in St. Peter's square, it was he who I had in mind, he and all whose dedicated lives wove that fabric we call Church. Kissing the Pope's Fisher Ring was my way of giving a kiss to each and every one of them.

What is your own experience of CHURCH? Where does God's Household become a tangible reality for you? How does it become most readily accessible? For many of my friends, this happens through Alcoholics Anonymous. "There," they say, "we come together in our shared dependence on a power greater than ourselves"—on "God as we understand Him." Jesus, if he walked among us today, might feel more at home in an AA meeting than in a great cathedral. In what community do you feel at home?

The Communion of Saints

❦

What does this really mean?

The Creed continues here along the same thread of faith in the Holy Spirit and in the Church (as a community that the Spirit inspires). Church is a community of *sharing*—which is the theme of this section—and of *healing*—which is the theme of the next.

From early on in the history of the Apostles' Creed, COMMUNION OF SAINTS has had a twofold meaning: Communion *realized among* the Saints, and Communion *celebrated by* the Saints. The Latin original—*communio sanctorum*—signifies both "sharing among holy people" and "sharing of holy things."

COMMUNION OF SAINTS can mean a community of holy *people* (holy not necessarily because they have achieved moral excellence, but because they are consecrated to God, like a holy temple). In this sense the term is synonymous with *Church*, but it emphasizes those aspects that go beyond the Church's visible manifestation. Most of those who pray the Creed today have this meaning in mind. The early Christians referred to all members of the Church as "Saints"; they are made holy by *belonging* to a holy community in the Holy Spirit. This community links not only different parts of the world, but, since the essential bond between its members is the life of Christ hidden in God's eternal Now, it transcends time and links all periods of history. According to Saint Augustine, the Church begins with Adam and Eve and endures to the very end of time. The upshot is limitless belonging.

COMMUNION OF SAINTS can also mean community through sharing of holy *things*. In this sense it is synonymous with *Holy*

Communion—the Eucharist, the celebration of the Lord's Supper. Today this meaning of the phrase has been almost forgotten; it can make a great difference, however, to remember it again in praying the Creed, for it emphasizes a dynamic aspect of community: *sharing*. Through the ritual sharing of bread and wine in the Eucharist, Christians communicate—in and through Christ—with one another and with God. But this sharing is open-ended because the community that celebrates it is all-embracing; it overflows into works of mercy. The upshot is limitless sharing.

Wherever there is true belonging and genuine sharing, God is present. In this sense faith in THE COMMUNION OF SAINTS goes far beyond its Christian frame of reference and has significance for the whole human community. We all belong together, therefore we must share. And when we do so, no matter how small the gesture—say, a black child sharing a cookie with a white child on the playground—that mind-boggling dimension of reality opens up, of which Kabir, the fifteenth-century Indian mystic, speaks as "the Holy One slowly growing a body."

How do we know this is so?

To answer this question, we need to focus on three points:

1. We know what we mean by Holy Spirit: the divine life within us and within the whole universe.
2. We know what we mean by Church: the community (beyond space and time) of those who are led by the Spirit.
3. We know that humans have a deep-rooted urge to celebrate community through the sharing of food. Wherever on earth people break bread together or drink from the same cup we know they express their belonging together.

On the basis of these three points, we know also a shared meal is the perfect expression of a community's life in the Spirit—its sacrament. A sacrament is a symbolic action manifesting what it signifies. The sacred meal to which the Creed refers as THE COMMUNION OF SAINTS brings about what it signifies: limitless COMMUNION with God's people of all times and places, in and through the Holy Spirit. The sacred meals of all times and places point toward this all-surpassing sharing and belonging.

Why make such a point of this?

Sharing and belonging—belonging through sharing, and sharing as celebration of belonging—find their most intense, most sacred Christian expression in the ritual meal called *Eucharist*, which means "thanksgiving." This grateful breaking of bread and passing of the cup constitutes the central ritual of the Christian community and goes back to its earliest beginnings. It connects today's community, breaking bread together, with Jesus—spiritually, because it takes place in the eternal Now, as well as historically. Table-fellowship was central to the community that Jesus gathered around himself, and its tradition has continued unbroken to this day. The distinctive mark of Jesus' table-fellowship was its inclusiveness. More than once did he get into trouble for "eating with sinners" (e.g., Matthew 9:10–13). Only if no one is excluded from our own table can we claim to celebrate Eucharist in his name and trust that he is "in the midst of us" (Matthew 18:20).

About theological interpretations of Christ's presence in our midst the Creed says nothing. Compared to the lived experience of sacred COMMUNION, abstract speculations count for little. They inevitably use the terms of one or another theological or philosophical genre, terms that are bound to a particular historical epoch and a particular geographic area. In contrast, the experience of a divine Presence in a sacred meal is and has been accessible to all humans always and everywhere.

COMMUNION in all its aspects is what our alienated, individualistic society most needs, most longs for. All who bravely step across social, racial, economic, or denominational demarcation lines in order to share generously and celebrate joyfully together, those are the ones who are truly in communion with Jesus Christ, whether they recognize him or not (see Matthew 25:35ff); they are the ones whom the Creed calls SAINTS.

Personal reflections

A moment of communion that is still vivid in my memory goes back to the days when outraged citizens still protested in the streets against the proliferation of nuclear arms. Tens of thousands gathered that morning near the UN headquarters in New York City to demonstrate in front of the embassies of nations possessing nuclear weapons. Our group went to the French embassy. It was a peaceful demonstration. Breaking Bread was our theme—the shared meal as the very antithesis of nuclear slaughter and devastation. "One bread, one body," we sang, and offered home-baked bread to everyone who passed by. Hungry street people helped themselves to whole loaves; we had brought plenty to go around. Father John Giuliani's genius for creating lively liturgy cast its spell even over the well-dressed ones hurrying to some office or meeting. Some were reluctant, but in my memory that Manhattan streetcorner is vibrant with morning sunlight, with the fragrance of freshly baked bread, and with the joyful tunes of communion songs—"Take and eat!"

Police, the visors of their helmets lowered, had closed ranks to prevent us from blocking the entrance to the embassy. A small, slightly stooped man in a gray business suit and tie—obviously a staff member—was just about to enter the building when he stopped and surveyed the scene. He looked like a mousy little fellow, but at this moment he caught on to what was at stake here. He looked down the line of police, looked over toward the singers, the banners, the bread baskets, and, straightening himself up, he suddenly seemed to grow taller. "I'd like to share this bread," he said with a strong voice. Never will I forget the joy in his eyes as he partook of this communion.

———

And you? When and where have you experienced sacramental sharing—sacramental in the sense of a sign or gesture that makes real what it signifies? When true communion happens, it is always Holy Communion, whether we are aware of it or not—communion with the kind of surpassing aliveness that alone can feed our deepest hunger. Can you think of ways to make this happen in your own surroundings and in your daily life?

The Forgiveness of Sins

―◄―

What does this really mean?

In order to spell out what THE FORGIVENESS OF SINS means, it is necessary to be clear about the concept of sin. Both sin and forgiveness are often misunderstood.

In today's English, "alienation" expresses most precisely the correct meaning of "sin" and avoids entanglement in unfortunate associations. SIN, rightly understood, is alienation from who we really are, our authentic Self, through identification with a mask; it is by the same stroke alienation from the world around us (people as well as environment); and SIN is also alienation from the divine Ground of our being. SIN in this sense is a condition rather than a particular sinful action. Any action—or failure to act—that springs from alienation or leads to alienation is also called "sin." We need to distinguish between SIN as action (or sinful *in*action!) and sin as condition, although these two are inseparably connected. If we fail to make this distinction, we will be apt to pay attention only to personal transgressions of dos and don'ts, and overlook our—often far graver—complicity in an alienation that pervades and poisons whole systems; this is SIN as the impersonal momentum of an alienated world.

The opposite of alienation is belonging. FORGIVENESS reestablishes belonging on all levels. Any refusal to belong, any exclusivity, causes a rift in the fabric of the cosmos in which all belong together with all. Forgiveness heals these rifts. It is more than pardon for transgressions; it restores communion. As the *for-* in FORGIVENESS (or the *per-* in the Latin *perdonare*) indicates, forgiving is an intensive form of giving. It demands from us the ultimate act of giving: *self*-giving. Only by letting go of our little ego with its resentments and vindictiveness can we come home to our true Self like the "prodigal Son" in the Gospel parable. When he finally hit the bottom of alienation "in an alien land," the parable tells us, "he came to himself," and this was the turning point. A heartbeat later he was on the road home to his father.

If we know that God is love and love is forgiveness, we know that God has forgiven "before always" all there ever was to forgive. In light of this we can let go of resenting our past. We can let go of remorse. Regret is healthy, remorse is not. The root meaning of *regret* has to do with tears, that of *remorse* with biting. Remorse suggests the compulsion of a dog to keep gnawing on his sore leg and make it worse. The tears of regret wash a festering wound and help it heal. W. B. Yeats vividly conveys what happens when we cast out remorse: "So great a sweetness flows into the breast," he says, that "we must laugh and we must sing," for we realize that "we are blest by everything, everything we look upon is blest." At that point we want to share the joy of love and forgiveness with the whole world. Joy has power to heal. Joyous faith in having received FORGIVENESS has the power to overcome alienation and nourish the peace that springs from a sense of belonging.

Just as faith in THE COMMUNION OF SAINTS finds its sacramental expression in the Eucharist, so the sacramental expression of THE FORGIVENESS OF SINS is Baptism. This ritual immersion in water signifies both death and birth. Water has this twofold significance, since we can drown in it and yet need it as a basic condition for life. Baptism signifies death to alienation and birth into our true home, the God Household. It is the homecoming from "an alien land" to our deepest belonging.

Baptism and Eucharist. How significant that the Creed refers to these two sacraments in the context of faith in the Holy Spirit. Real faith shows itself in radical commitment to action. Radical commitment to sharing can make any meal a Eucharist. "For where two or three come together in my name, there am I with them" (Matthew 18:20). Radical commitment to the healing of alienation in one's own life and in the world at large is what the Christian tradition calls Baptism of Desire. It can take the place of sacramental FORGIVENESS OF SINS and unites non-Christians and Christians alike in THE COMMUNION OF SAINTS.

How do we know this is so?

The first step toward an understanding of THE FORGIVENESS OF SINS is an effort to learn what SIN and FORGIVENESS mean in the context of the Creed. The second step consists of translating these terms into a language that can be understood today and does not push too many alarm buttons. We have tried this earlier by suggesting *alienation* and *healing* as terms that convey the full meaning but are less loaded than *sin* and *forgiveness*. Both steps are necessary before one can with integrity understand, appreciate, and recite the Creed.

Every mature person knows the feeling of alienation—from oneself, from others, and from one's Ultimate Reference Point of Belonging (a bit clumsy, but not a bad substitute for the term *God* if you are allergic to it). We can also become aware that these are merely three different dimensions of one and the same state of alienation. For example, no one can say, "I have been a bit alienated from myself lately, but my relationships with others are just fine." We also know from experience that healing forgiveness is of one piece, whether it begins with forgiving others, ourselves, or a God whom we blame as if God were "someone else." When we let go of our little ego and return home to our true Self, we find God there—closer to us than we are to ourselves. Not only has God forgiven us "before always," but, as the great mystic Julian of Norwich stated, God cares for the sinner with double love, like a mother for a child who has fallen and hurts. This, too, we know in our heart of hearts.

Why make such a point of this?

Faith in THE FORGIVENESS OF SINS is still an implication of faith in God as Holy Spirit. One after the other, the Creed unfolds these implications. The Spirit establishes community (the CHURCH) and celebrates community (COMMUNION) as a healing community (FORGIVENESS). Since in this clause of the Creed the emphasis is on the healing of *all* alienation, world-community comes into focus. Nothing could be more urgent today. Faith in THE FORGIVENESS OF SINS constitutes a commitment to work for a just society at peace with the environment.

This peace and this justice are not at all the same as "law and order." The latter phrase, in current parlance, suggests a society in which swift retaliation against behavior that departs from the norm and tough punishment of offenders protect the status quo. Can we imagine a radically different society? FORGIVENESS goes to the roots and starts reform from there. A society built on FORGIVENESS would realize that an individual's crimes are often the result of a malfunctioning system; it would strike at the roots of deviant behavior by building not bigger and bigger prisons but better and better schools. When we ask how FORGIVENESS might change the world-community, we should remember that the words "forgive us as we forgive" in the Lord's Prayer referred originally not to sins but to debts. International Debt Remission comes to mind, with the ironic twist that the "sinners"—offenders against justice and peace—are in this case not the debtors but the lenders turned exploiters.

All concrete situations pose intricate practical problems. It would be simplistic to claim that FORGIVENESS *is* the solution or *has* the solution. But we can say that it offers the most promising approach to finding solutions, for two reasons: first, a forgiving attitude springs from a sense of belonging, and so it tackles the root of injustice, which is alienation; second (for-giving being the most demanding giving—self-giving), it gives itself wholeheartedly to finding a solution to the problem at hand, without hiding behind legalism. The Romans, from whom our own legal system derives, knew already: *Summa ius, summa iniuria*—"extreme justice is extreme injustice" (Cicero). The opposite of "law and order" is not lawlessness and chaos, but peace built on forgiveness and justice built on belonging. Through faith that FORGIVENESS shall overcome all alienation in the power of the Spirit, the notion of CHURCH is broadened to include all who are committed to this goal.

Personal reflections

It has been said humans are never more beautiful than when they ask for forgiveness, or forgive others. When we feel guilty, however, all we can see is the wrong we have done, and we feel its burden. Who has not experienced this?

To me it seemed as if the weight of a mountain had fallen on my conscience when I had swung once too often on the lowest limb of our landlord's cherry tree. The loud crack with which the branch snapped sounded to me like the thunder of Judgment Day. To hide was my first impulse, but there was no hiding place. My two brothers and I tried to lift the hanging-down branch back into position and tie it back to the splintered stump, but we soon realized how stupid and futile our attempts were. I knew I'd have to 'fess up to what I had done and ask forgiveness, but I couldn't get myself to face that task—not yet, at any rate. Maybe there was some way out. The longer I waited, the heavier I felt the burden of my guilt. After all, we had generously been granted the run of the garden and were even allowed to climb the trees, only swinging on the branches was forbidden.

Finally, I was on my way upstairs to where our landlord lived, but still I was dragging my heels. Or rather it felt as if I—*some* I—were dragging myself—some *other* I—up the stairs, one tread at a time. The scene engraved itself on my memory like a film in slow motion. Our landlord's figure, tall and haggard, filled the doorframe as I stood there mumbling my confession. If the roof had fallen in at that moment, it would not have surprised me—in fact, it would have been a relief. Herr Engineer Baumgartner was known to be a man of few words. *"Oy weh!"* he said. Just that: *"Oy weh!"* and quite expressionless at that. But then, as I looked up at him, he gave me a broad smile. I think he also ruffled my hair with his heavy hand. But the smile was the great gift with which he sent me away, the gift of forgiveness.

Can you remember an occasion when you received this gift—or gave it? Nowhere more clearly than with regard to forgiveness are we humans the carriers of God's gifts, and the sowers of God's seed for a harvest of peace. Perhaps that is the reason humans are never more beautiful than when they beg forgiveness or forgive: they are radiant with the beauty of God's own inexhaustible forgiveness.

Do you find it difficult to leave behind the Sunday-school notion of sin as a spot on your soul? In what way does an understanding of sin as alienation and of FORGIVENESS as healing-through-belonging help you to deal with conflict situations in your daily living? Can you apply the distinction between remorse and regret to the way you deal with memories of failure? When have you experienced an outstanding example of FORGIVENESS given or received?

The Resurrection of the Body

~

What does this really mean?

The meaning of RESURRECTION OF THE BODY follows from the placement of this clause within the Creed. We are still unpacking here what faith in the Holy Spirit implies. All along in this part of the Creed, the key concept is *belonging*. The Spirit "holds all things together," as the Wisdom of Solomon puts it (1:7). The Buddhist monk Thich Nhat Hanh calls this universal belonging "Interbeing." Everything is within everything else, because the whole is brought forth and animated by one and the same Life-breath of God.

In the preceding sections of the Creed we saw this belonging expressed in a community (CHURCH) that is called together by the Spirit (HOLY), all-embracing (CATHOLIC), supportive and nourishing (COMMUNION), and healing (FORGIVENESS). As we shall see now, this present tenet follows the same thread of thought and leads to a cosmic view of belonging. More immediately, however, faith in THE RESURRECTION OF THE BODY evokes personal concerns—*my* body and *my* life beyond death. We shall therefore begin with this personal focus.

Here, too, belonging is the key to understanding what is meant. My body belongs to me not as some optional appendix to my self-awareness, but as its embodiment. It belongs to me, not in the sense in which my clothes belong to me, but rather as sound belongs to a song. I am somebody; I *am* my body. And yet, not long ago, every atom of this physical body was part of some other living or nonliving entity, and will be so again before long. Even now, every single second, millions of red blood cells die and are replaced by new ones—and so, at different rates, with all the other cells in my body. What remains unchanged has been called "the inner body," or "the soul." My friends still recognize me after every physical component of me has died and been replaced (which supposedly happens every seven years or so) because of this unchanging "soul." This identity of mine is the unique expression of Life in and through me—not the little life span that belongs to me, but that great reservoir of Life to which I belong. Unlike a battery-run toy animal, I am permanently connected to a universal power grid that is inexhaustible—the Holy Spirit that "fills the whole universe" (Wisdom of Solomon 1:7).

Forms arise and dissolve like soap bubbles, but the Spirit brings them forth, the Breath of God shapes and fills them, and therefore every single one of them is infinitely precious and sacred. "Just to *be* is a blessing; just to *live* is holy," said the great rabbi Abraham Heschel. Once in a while our eyes pop open and we look through the form to its holy identity. Think, for example, of young parents enthralled by every tiny toenail, every smallest hair of their first baby. In such moments we are awestruck by the vision and overwhelmed by the blessing of sheer being.

On that deepest level, Life simply *is*—Being simply *is*—beneath the comings and goings of forms. In the Gospel of John, Jesus refers to this deepest level when he says, "I have come that they may have life, and have it to the full" (10:10). In his own life he breathed the imperishable Life-breath of God, and *this* life cannot perish, not even in death. Saint Paul assures us that this is true of us, too: "If the Spirit of the one who raised Jesus from the dead dwells in you, the one who raised Christ from the dead will give life to your mortal bodies also, through his Spirit dwelling in you" (Romans 8:11).

Because Jesus allowed the power of the Holy Spirit to shape his life, his end was not death and destruction, but—in, through, and beyond death—life in God. In the same way, all who follow the lead of the Spirit are headed ultimately not toward death, but toward RESURRECTION. All their spirit-filled bodily reality will be "hidden with Christ in God" (Colossians 3:3). This is a different image of THE RESURRECTION OF THE BODY from the medieval one of revived corpses struggling out of their tombs on Doomsday, but it, too, is merely an image. We have to respect the limits of our imagination. In this phrase of the Creed we proclaim our trust in dimensions beyond our imagination. Our true Life here and now—in all its bodily fullness—is beyond the power of death, because it is participation in the life of God.

Here our focus widens from personal concerns to a cosmic perspective. Through our bodies we belong inextricably to all other living beings; all atoms in our flesh and bones have once been in a supernova. What this tenet of the Creed proclaims speaks not only of our human bodies, but of all *flesh* (which is the original word, now replaced by BODY); it includes all forms that vanish in time— the whole universe. All beings, no matter how ephemeral, are brought forth by God's Spirit and loved by God with unimaginable fervor and tenderness. Jesus asked, "Are not five sparrows sold for two pennies?" and he assured his disciples, "Yet not one of them is forgotten by God" (Luke 12:6). Since God remembers this sparrow, its brief, twittering life can never be lost. Only in time can anything pass away. But when time itself will long have passed away, all that looked so fleeting from the perspective of time—every twitter of that sparrow—will be found in all its morning freshness in God's eternal Now. That Now is beyond time, but we experience it in time moment by moment, refracted, as it were, the way white light is refracted color by color. This can give great consolation to all who mourn the death of a loved one, for there, beyond time, we shall find our friends, our relatives, our pets—and of course also those with whom we can't get along; so, better to make peace with them right now.

Ultimately, the meaning of THE RESURRECTION OF THE BODY hinges on the notion of belonging: "All things belong to you, and you belong to Christ; and Christ belongs to God" (1 Corinthians 3:22f)—and whatever belongs to God belongs to indestructible Being.

How do we know this is so?

How can we possibly have experiential knowledge of THE RESUR-
RECTION OF THE BODY? Unlike all other tenets of the Creed, this one
points to an event that has not yet happened. On what can we base
our assumption that this is a trustworthy assertion? Before we are
ready to answer this question, some introspection is necessary. By
focusing our full attention within, we can become aware that our "I
am" does not depend on our "I think." When we manage to stop
thinking for a brief moment—and stay alert—we experience our inner being beyond thought. We find ourselves rooted in Being, of which
the myriad of beings—our own little self included—are so many fleeting expressions. Beings come and go, they arise and vanish, but our
innermost actuality is Being itself, the permanent ground of all im-
permanent forms. This is decisive. It needs to be stressed. Deep inner awareness of indestructible Being is accessible to any human
being. But how could we be aware of this indestructibility without
participating in it? Our innermost being is indestructible, although
we cannot imagine what this will mean for us when our temporal
form is dissolved. The syllable *re-* in RE-SURRECTION OF THE BODY
is borrowed from time-bound imagery; to cling to it would be misleading. Imagination fails us when we experience a reality beyond
time. Awareness *that* we belong to indestructible Being is a weighty
fact, even though we do not know *how* this will play itself out.

Sometimes this awareness rushes in on us as an overwhelming
surprise. In our most genuinely alive moments (Abraham Maslow's
peak experiences), we become aware of a life-force within us that
is not subject to decay. In these moments we experience what
Maslow calls the B-values—facets of the diamond of Being—
beauty, truth, goodness, and the like. You may look at (and smell)
an orchard in full bloom, listen to David Whyte reciting a poem of
profound truth, or watch firefighters on the evening news, and suddenly you experience with a shiver of recognition that your own life
is indestructible because it is animated by the beautiful, true, good,
and indestructible life-force.

This being-in-the-flow of Life, this being-accurately-set-right with Being, goes also by the names of *righteousness* and *justice*. When we catch a glimpse of it, when we get the slightest taste of it, we understand intuitively what Psalm 16:9 wants to say: "You [God] will not let your righteous one see corruption." In our peak moments, too, the wholeness and integrity we sense is not merely mental, but includes the body. "My body of a sudden blazed," writes W. B. Yeats about one of his peak experiences ("Vacillation," verse IV). He experienced the radiance of his inner body. In our best moments we are aware that we are (mind *and* body) rooted in Being, one with Life itself.

The experience of our mortality does not invalidate the insights we gain from high points of aliveness. Dying and living belong together, but Life is bigger than both. We know from experience that living is inseparable from dying—not only at the end, but throughout. Moment by moment we have to let go of the old, in order to come alive to the new. These many little deaths are a training process, as it were, for our last death. Faith is trust in this inner dynamic of Life—in the Holy Spirit. This faith gives us confidence that in our last moment, just as in every other, the letting go of an old aliveness will make us ready to receive the new—in this case a hitherto unimagined aliveness.

Why make such a point of this?

It is a weighty matter to appreciate not only the dignity of the body, but the ultimate dignity of bodily existence. This appreciation presupposes a certain degree of maturity. It takes time to develop this maturity—not only in our personal lives, but in the lives of whole societies and cultures. In the first enthusiasm of discovering Spirit as something radiating beyond bodily reality, the tendency is to belittle everything else as merely material and perishable, and even to despise it. Only gradually do we become aware of the importance of distinguishing between these two inseparable realms.

To neglect either Spirit or body has detrimental consequences for both. Disembodied spirit becomes impotent. Bodily reality, separate from Spirit, loses its dignity and falls prey to abuse. Rape of the environment is shocking proof of this artificial and untenable separation. Ascetics of all traditions have often gone too far, mistreating their bodies instead of seeing them as temples of the Holy Spirit. They sought to strengthen the Spirit by weakening the body, as if the body were not a tool of the Spirit, but an enemy. The body may be hard to handle at times, but without this tool, what could we accomplish? How could we serve the crying needs around us?

On the other hand, when the body is no longer tool and expression of the Spirit within it, how can it thrive? It is one and the same life-force that drives our bodily appetites and guides us toward our loftiest goals. Deprived of this guidance, our body resembles a runaway car. It careens into abuse of every kind. In any 12-step meeting you will hear life stories that illustrate and prove this point.

The same abuse we inflict on our bodies when we no longer experience them as embodiment of Spirit, we perpetrate on our environment when we forget that it, too, is alive with divine life-force. Imagine how different our world would look if we recognized Earth as our wider bodily existence. We reverence and cherish every form of life the moment we become aware that it is animated by the divine Spirit. Faith in THE RESURRECTION OF THE BODY is intimately bound up with reverence for the whole cosmos.

Personal reflections

As a psychology student in post–World War II Vienna, I landed an enviable job. I was hired as Prefect (a sort of mixture between a tutor and a surrogate mother) for the Vienna Boys' Choir. At that time the choir was still housed in the same thick-walled tract of the Imperial Palace in Vienna that had been the boys' living quarters at the time of Christopher Columbus when Emperor Maximilian I established the choir in 1498. In summer, however, they moved to their vacation home at Hinterbichl, high in the Alps of the Eastern

Tyrol. Here I had an experience that always comes to mind when someone asks me about THE RESURRECTION OF THE BODY.

While the boys had their choir practice, I was enjoying some free time and had climbed up a steep path to a high lookout point. Surrounded by the stillness of the snow-covered peaks, I heard from deep down below the strains of one of my favorite pieces, da Vittoria's motet "Duo Seraphim." The text speaks of two angels afire with adoration, calling out, one to the other, "Holy, holy, holy!"

It was as if the wings of my soul had brushed against the Everlasting. I find it impossible to put into words what this did to me. That moment shaped my deepest self. Those silver voices blended with my own innermost cry: Holy, holy, holy! I knew that this voice was imperishable, and it was my own voice, the perfect and total expression of who I was—not in some abstract way, but rock-bottom real. The smallest detail of that scene, every dewdrop of that July morning, every slightest modulation of the voices rising through the mountain air was impressed as with a divine branding iron, not on my memory so much as on my very being.

My memory may fade, or be erased. But when time is up for me, and only Now remains, I will be in the Now of that summer morning—and of course in *every* Now of my lifetime. Nothing is lost, no matter how fleeting it may appear, for "all is always now" (T. S. Eliot). I believe in THE RESURRECTION OF THE FLESH (why limit myself to the BODY?), and this means I trust that *all* that is fleeting and perishable is, nevertheless, preserved in its pristine freshness in the one eternal Now. It need not be brought back from the dust like the bodies in medieval representations of Judgment Day, because it is—with the risen Christ—"hidden in God." This is why I trust that we will see our loved ones with every dimple and every freckle that was dear to us, when we "see God."

If you have ever deeply loved, you know what I mean. At my age you can look at photographs of relatives you have known from birth to death. Your love embraces that baby in the tub no less than the smile of the first-grader with the missing tooth, the teenager on a bike or dressed up for the prom, and image after image down to that last wan smile. In which one do you see the person you loved? In each and all of them. You need not make a choice. Every moment of life is present in "the now that does not pass away"—that means, in eternity. The poet Rainer Maria Rilke thought that it was our essential task as human beings to harvest, like busy bees, the nectar of the visible world into the great golden honeycomb of the invisible.

That morning in the Tyrolean Alps and the "Holy, holy, holy!" of the two seraphim is not just preserved as memory trace in a brain destined to rot. It is engraved on my imperishable Self. When the drop of water that is my life falls back into the ocean, it will carry the flavor of da Vittoria's "Duo Seraphim" and add it to all the waters of the sea, never ever to be lost.

And you? Is the body—your own and the body of someone you love—important enough to you that the idea of some disembodied afterlife holds little appeal? Did you ever become so strongly aware of your imperishable Self that the thought no longer upsets you that your brain and your body will be dust before too long? How does watching a series of photographs of someone you loved—as child, as youth, as adult, in old age—affect you? How does the fact that "all is always now" affect your understanding of THE RESURRECTION OF THE BODY?

And Life Everlasting

~

What does this really mean?

Faith in LIFE EVERLASTING still belongs to that part of the Creed that started with I BELIEVE IN THE HOLY SPIRIT. Spirit *is* LIFE, and faith in life is the culmination of faith in the Spirit.

EVERLASTING is a misleading translation of this phrase in the original text of the Creed. It suggests interminable time, while the Latin *vitam aeternam* could be more accurately translated as "life beyond time," that is, life freed from the limitations of time. The word *aeternus* comes from a root that signifies vibrant vitality. Thus, rightly understood, EVERLASTING wants to remind us not of the flowers by that name often used in wreaths and in dry flower arrangements, but rather of a meadow full of spring flowers or, to change the metaphor, of an eternal Fountain of Youth, ever flowing, ever fresh, ever new. These are qualities of life in the Spirit, an aliveness we can experience at any given moment, just by breathing deeply and mindfully.

This article of the Creed does not tie us down to any particular imagery or theory of "afterlife." It is not concerned with "after," but expresses a joyful commitment to "Life in fullness" (John 10:10). The life to which we joyfully commit ourselves in this final clause of the Creed is not tied to any "before" or "after," but is freed from enslavement to past and future. We celebrate this LIFE here—wherever we may be—and in the great Now that dissolves time.

How do we know this is so?

The original text of the Creed leads up to the glorious affirmation of ETERNAL LIFE—*vitam aeternam*. What a pity our English translation speaks of LIFE EVERLASTING. Doesn't this sound as if our current time-bound life were to go on forever and ever? What a nightmare! Fortunately, ETERNAL LIFE means life freed from the shackles of time. Nor do we have to wait for this liberation until we die. Kabir, the fifteenth-century mystic, asks:

> *If you don't break your ropes while you're alive*
> *do you think*
> *ghosts will do it after?*

If death means that time is over for me, what could "after" mean, anyway? In the Creed we do not profess faith in life *after* death, but *beyond* death. This is not a denial of "life after death"; rather it is infinitely more of an affirmation because it takes the "after" out of that phrase. Whether we are aware of it or not, life-beyond-death is what we truly long for. And we do not have to wait for it. We can break our ropes today. We can go beyond time—beyond death—to the extent to which we live in the Now.

At certain peak moments in life, when we are awake and alive on every level of our being, we can experience a certain timelessness. An hour may go by and seem like a brief moment; the clock may go on ticking, but for us time stands still. In those moments we touch, as it were, eternity, which Saint Augustine calls "the Now that does not pass away"—*nunc stans*, in his elegant Latin two-word definition. We know eternity, because in our best moments we experience ourselves as free from the restrictions of time. The more we learn to live in the Now (which embraces past and future), the more we come alive. Anyone can test this by experience. This aliveness goes beyond our limited existence within space and time—there is more and ever more to it—and so we ascribe it to transcendent Spirit. Even a glimpse of it suffices to make us aware that death has no power over it. Our whole being longs for this aliveness.

Why make such a point of this?

The whole Creed leads up to this climax: "Life in Fullness" (John 10:10). Whatever could be named as being important to us humans is contained in this phrase. In every single phrase of the Creed we have committed ourselves to this divine LIFE, and in the final one we make this commitment explicit. Thus, this last phrase refers back to "Father," to God as Source of Life, to "Son" as the Human who lives this life so fully that even "death is swallowed up in victory" (1 Corinthians 15:54), and to "Spirit" as the ever-young divine Vitality within us—within the universe. These three notes, struck separately in the three sections of the Creed, sound together as a final chord in the word LIFE.

Personal reflections

To illustrate this, let me tell you about a dramatic moment when the choice between time and now demanded a split-second decision from me. The setting was dramatic in its own way—the former Flagler mansion in Palm Beach, Florida, home of the Apollo Boys' Choir, with whom I lived as a counselor after my time with the Vienna Boys' Choir. Emery Moore's alto voice was outstanding even among the many fine voices in this choir, but he had reached the age when it would soon break. There was no hope that his boy's voice would last another season. The evening breeze from the ocean played with the curtains in the high-arched windows, amber light set the room aglow, Emery stood by the piano, and one more time his mellow voice intoned Handel's aria "O Had I Jubal's Lyre."

The recording equipment stood ready. A flick of my finger could catch these honey-golden notes on tape, but no; I left them their freedom, and they soared like birds.

Fully present, I was able to experience that music beyond time, to allow it to give wings to my heart in the eternal Now. By refusing to make it "everlasting"—whatever that means, anyway—I discovered that it belonged to my ETERNAL LIFE. I heard it with the imperishable ear of my heart.

And you? What are your hopes for life beyond death? (Notice, I did not say "*after* death," for that would place it in time. When our time is up, we go *beyond* time into the Now. Of course we don't have to wait until our last hour to experience the Now.) When, where, and how do you personally experience the Now most clearly and strongly? Can you remember what T. S. Eliot called a "moment in and out of time"? Can you relate that experience to LIFE EVERLASTING?

Amen

~

What does this really mean?

It is helpful to consider the concluding AMEN as an integral part of the Creed. Otherwise, it could too easily become a mere embellishment, like the flourish under a signature.

The root meaning of AMEN is faithfulness, reliability. AMEN expresses human trust in God's trustworthiness. Thus the last word of the Creed echoes the first—*Credo*, I give my heart to the One I trust. All the statements of the Creed between these two words are variations on this theme; each of them affirms human faith in divine faithfulness. The final AMEN sums them all up and imprints on them the seal of personal commitment.

Since AMEN is typically a response of the whole community to God's Word—to the faithful Presence that the worshipping community encounters—this final AMEN places the faith of the one who proclaims it into a communal context. The first word of the Creed was *I*; the last one reverberates with the *we* of community.

We can visualize this community in widening circles. The narrowest one consists of Christians, in whose language, after all, the Creed is formulated. But Jews and Muslims also sum up their faith in the same word AMEN. Thus the three Amen-traditions of the West, together, form a wider circle of shared faith. Moreover, AMEN is related to *Aum* or *Om*, the sacred syllable of a still wider community. Among Hindus, Jains, and Buddhists, *Om* also expresses assent and blessing, and links the one who pronounces it in faith with the ultimate horizon of human existence, just as AMEN does.

How do we know this is so?

A good example for the original Hebrew use of AMEN is the fourteen-times repeated "And all the people shall say 'Amen,' " in Deuteronomy 27:15–26. And for the traditions of the East, the Mandukya Upanishad sets the tone: it is in its entirety devoted to speculations regarding *Om,* which it considers the greatest of all mantras.

Beyond this external information, however, we can experience the power of AMEN by listening to its musical setting at the end of the Creed, say, in Bach's B minor Mass. Even the five-times repeated AMEN, popularized by Sidney Poitier in the film *Lilies of the Field*, conveys some mysterious power. In India, today, Yagadguru Ramanandacharya has made *Om* the focus of his teachings and helps his students to experience in it "the sound of God."

Why make such a point of this?

Our understanding of AMEN reflects our approach to the whole Creed: to find a deeper significance in Christian faith by experiencing it in a universal human context. Throughout our reflections on the Creed we have tried to dig down to the roots of basic human faith—the trust in Life we share with all our brothers and sisters in the human family—and from this perspective to understand the particular Christian expression of that shared faith.

The less we insist on the specific expression that Christian tradition has given to human faith, the less we try to make this one form the only one, the easier it becomes to appreciate its depth, its beauty, its uniqueness displayed in the Apostles' Creed. In Beethoven's Ninth Symphony we hear the famous melody to Schiller's "Ode to Joy" first softly, almost inaudibly, in the bass section, but gradually one instrument after another will take it up and even the chorus of human voices will join in and repeat it triumphantly. In a similar way, each spiritual tradition takes up the theme of faith and gives it expression in its own voice, through its own particular beliefs.

Our instrument may be the cello or the oboe, but we will appreciate the melody we play all the more by hearing all the other instruments of the orchestra give it voice in their own particular way. Only the full orchestra of the world's spiritual traditions can adequately sound out the AMEN of human faith in response to God's faithfulness.

Personal reflections

More than eight thousand people had gathered in Chicago in August 1993 for the Parliament of the World's Religions. They came from all over the globe and represented a great diversity of religious traditions. At the original Parliament of the World's Religions in 1893, Chicago had become the birthplace of worldwide formal interreligious dialogue. Ever since, this dialogue had gathered momentum, but only now, exactly a hundred years later, was the world ready for a second Parliament to convene. Today this historic moment had arrived, and here I was in Chicago, privileged beyond my wildest dreams with an invitation to help shape this event. The atmosphere was charged with excitement, but the question of what to say to so august a gathering did not let me sleep that night.

Two things were clear to me: what I would say had to faithfully represent my own Catholic Christian tradition, *and* I had to make myself understood by all the other traditions. This meant that I had to speak from the heart of my own tradition to the heart of all others. The heart of the Christian tradition is clearly faith in the Blessed Trinity—God as Father, Son, and Holy Spirit. How could I hope to be understood by sisters and brothers from other traditions when I spoke about this innermost core of Christian faith? Could they find an access route to it? And if so, how? Thus the question that kept me awake that night became more sharply focused: Was mutual understanding in interfaith dialogue at all possible when it came to the most distinctive beliefs of disparate spiritual traditions?

This question was as bothersome as it was crucial. As I rolled it around and around in my mind that night, two phrases began to stand out: "inter*faith* dialogue" and "distinctive *beliefs*." We share faith, but beliefs get in the way of our deepest sharing. Our heart understands the inner gesture that all other human hearts make in faith, for faith is one. But beliefs are many, and our intellect grapples with differences that seem insurmountable. Faith unites us, beliefs divide us. Thus I would have to go deeper and ask, What is the relationship between faith and beliefs—between *my* faith and *my* beliefs? The answer was easy: My beliefs are the expression of my faith. When this dawned on me, my basic approach was clear. To find the starting point for mutual understanding, I had to go beyond the beliefs that divide us and appeal to the faith that unites us.

But what is this universal faith before it expresses itself in beliefs? How do we experience it? As you read these lines, try to answer that question for yourself. How and in what context do *you* experience your deepest trust in the trustworthiness of Life? My own answer emerged when I focused on the greatest challenge to my faith, the question, Is there meaning at all? In my darkest moments, I doubt it. Only courageous trust—and this is the essence of the most basic, most universal faith—can overcome the obstacle of universal doubt. Our universal human faith is the courage and trust we show by our common search for ultimate meaning.

The search for meaning is our common ground. When this became clear to me, I knew where I would take my stand when I addressed the Parliament of the World's Religions: what we have in common is our search for meaning, and so we must explore the basics of our shared experience of meaning together. Now a clear structure for my approach suggested itself. From whatever angle you approach it, meaning always shows three basic aspects: Word, Silence, and Understanding. If one is missing, we cannot experience meaning. So I would speak about our human search for meaning under the aspects of Word, Silence, and Understanding.

Word may be the most familiar of the three. Whenever we find a thing, person, or situation meaningful, we feel that it "speaks" to us. Thus, it is Word in the widest sense—not the kind of word you find in a dictionary, but word, nevertheless, because it conveys meaning. But every word that deserves that name comes out of silence—the heart of silence; only thus can it speak to the silence of the heart. (All else is chitchat.) Yet neither word nor silence alone can trigger the "aha!" of meaning; there must also be understanding. Understanding is a dynamic process. When we listen so deeply to a word that we allow it to lead us into the silence from whence it comes, understanding happens. Silence comes to word, and word, through understanding, returns into silence.

The delegates here at Chicago presented a colorful spectacle—from the saffron robes of Buddhist monks to the black ones of Eastern Christian monks; from the tall hats of Orthodox archimandrites to the yarmulkes of Jewish rabbis, the turbans of Sikhs, and the eagle-feather war bonnets of Native American chiefs. As my eyes delighted in this great variety, I knew that underlying all the outward trappings, the same longing for meaning was the inner force that had brought all these seekers here.

If every religious tradition is an expression of the human heart's perennial quest for meaning, then the three characteristic aspects of meaning—Word, Silence, and Understanding—must characterize every one of the world's religions. All three will be present in every tradition, for they are essential for meaning, yet we might expect to find differences of emphasis, and indeed we do find them. In the primal religions—Australian, African, or Native American, for instance—our three aspects of meaning are still quite equally emphasized and interwoven with one another in myth, ritual, and right living. But as Buddhism, Hinduism, and the Western traditions grow out of the primal religious matrix, emphasis in a given tradition will fall more strongly on Word, or Silence, or Understanding, although all three will always play their role in each tradition.

My conversations with Rabbi Joseph Geleberman, with Father Hans Kung, with Pir Vilayat Inayat Khan, had convinced me that in the Western traditions—Judaism, Christianity, and Islam—Word is central, because God is conceived as the One who speaks. God speaks to us through all there is, for everything is essentially a word of God. God's one creating and redeeming Word is spelled out to us in ever-new ways. God is love, and so God has nothing else to say in all eternity but "I love you!" Just as lovers never tire to express their love in gifts and songs and flowers and caresses, so God repeats "I love you" in ever-new ways through everything that comes into being.

But I had noticed that among my Buddhist teachers Silence held as central a place as Word does for us in the West. Nowhere does this become more obvious than in the account of the Buddha's great wordless sermon. How can there be a sermon without words? The Buddha simply holds up a flower. Only one of his disciples understands, it is said. But how can that one prove without a word that he understood? He smiles, the story tells us. The Buddha smiles back and in the silence between them the tradition is passed on from the Buddha to his first successor, the disciple with the understanding smile. Ever since, we are told, the tradition of Buddhism is passed on in silence. To put it more correctly, what is handed on—the tradition itself—is Silence. This explains what I had experienced with Eido Roshi. When I thought I had understood some aspect of Zen Buddhist teaching and checked this out with him, expressing my insight as clearly as I could, he would laugh and say, "Perfectly correct, but what a pity that you have to put it into words!" And when in our conversations he got carried away and explained a point, he would catch himself in the middle of a sentence and joke, "I have been talking again; I'm becoming a Christian."

Swami Satchidananda had already arrived in Chicago, and I had caught a glimpse of him. He was widely known as the Woodstock Guru. He had opened the Woodstock Festival in August 1969, billed as "three days of peace and music," by calling music "the celestial sound that controls the whole universe." From my long friendship with this great teacher I knew that in Hinduism, not Word or Silence, but Understanding, holds the central position. "Yoga *is* Understanding," says Swami Venkatesananda with deep insight into what makes Hinduism tick. Remember what we said about Understanding as the process by which Silence comes to Word and Word comes home into Silence. This gave me a clue to the central intuition of Hinduism: "Atman *is* Brahman"—God manifest (Word) is God un-manifest (Silence)—and "Brahman *is* Atman"—the divine Un-manifest (Silence) is the manifest divine (Word). To know that Word is Silence and Silence is Word—distinct without separation, and inseparable, yet without confusion—this is Understanding. (Of course I am referring to an existential understanding that goes infinitely beyond the grasp of the intellect.)

When, in our quest for meaning, we hit upon a great discovery, we typically exclaim, "This is it!" I decided to play with "this is it!" in my talk about faith and the human quest for ultimate meaning. The Christian perspective gives itself away by emphasizing the first word of this little sentence: *This* is it! Enthusiasm for the discovery that "God speaks" that everything is Word of God, makes us exclaim again and again, "*This* is it!" and "*This* is it!" whenever we are struck by another Word that reveals meaning. Not so with Buddhism. Buddhism is struck by the one Silence that comes to Word in so great a multitude and variety of words. "This is *it*," Buddhism exclaims; and this and this and this, every one of all these words, is always *it*, is always the one Silence-come-to-word. We need Hinduism to remind us that what really matters is that "this *is* it"— that Word *is* Silence and Silence *is* Word—therein lies true Understanding.

Eido Roshi used to chide his students: "You Westerners say that you want to under-stand, but you really want to *over*-stand. You are like people taking a shower with an umbrella up." In order to understand water, you have to get wet. Talking about water will not help you. Neither will making words about understanding explain it to anyone. Silence, Word, and Understanding cannot be translated into one another; we must respect their uniqueness as we respect the uniqueness of Buddhism, the Amen Traditions, and Hinduism. Their perspectives complement one another. By appreciating other perspectives, we learn to broaden our own without losing it. The traditions need one another's help in the quest for meaning.

But, if anywhere, it was here at the Parliament of the World's Religions that an important truth became obvious: religion is not only the *quest* for meaning, it is also the *celebration* of meaning. Every one of these glorious days here in Chicago would bring new festivities, new celebrations displaying the splendor of one tradition after the other. It was like a splendid spiritual party. The image of a great dance popped into my mind, and I decided to use this image in my address to the assembly.

As early as the fourth century, the Greek Fathers of the Church had used the image of a circle-dance (as when children dance, holding hands in a circle) in their theological reflections on the triune God: the Son—the Lord of the Dance—comes forth from the Father and returns in the Holy Spirit to the Father. If my Christian belief in God as triune—not one and not three, but one *as* three and three *as* one—was truly an expression of the faith I share with all other humans, then even so specific a belief as that in the Blessed Trinity must be contained—as seed—in universal human faith. And indeed in our quest for meaning we become aware that the Word comes forth from the Silence and returns through Understanding into the Silence. Thus all faith is in some sense Trinitarian. The "revelation" that at first glance had seemed to be unique to my Christian faith lay at the core of all faith and I could hope to reach other men and women of faith when I spoke from the Trinitarian core of my own tradition. This I was now determined to do.

I would speak of the human quest for meaning as a great circle-dance in which those who live by the Word hold hands with those who dive into the Silence and with those whose path is Understanding.

There is something intriguing about the image of a circle-dance. Just visualize it for a moment. As long as you stand outside of the circle, it will always seem to you that those nearest to you are going in one direction, those farthest away in exactly the opposite one.

There is no way of overcoming this illusion except by getting into the circle. As soon as you hold hands and become one of the dancers, you realize that all are going in the same direction. The moment I brought up this image in my talk, I saw that the audience caught on. It was one of the great moments in my life—a peak experience, an experience of limitless belonging, a taste of the Now that does not pass away. Looking out over this assembly of the world's religions, I could almost hear an AMEN arising from many hearts.

God is the faithfulness at the heart of all things, faith is our response to that faithfulness, and the one-word expression of that faith is AMEN. From the core of our being (the Christ in us) we say AMEN to Faithfulness (to God un-manifest), and saying AMEN is faith in action (the action of the Holy Spirit). Thus the very word AMEN reverberates with overtones of God as Trinity.

What else could dancers in the great circle-dance sing? "Amen, Amen—and sing it again—Amen!"

About the Author

BROTHER DAVID STEINDL-RAST is one of the best-known spiritual teachers in the world. Born in Austria in 1926, he came to the United States after receiving his Ph.D. in psychology from the University of Vienna. As a member of the Benedictine Order of Catholic monks, he is known for pioneering work in interfaith dialogue, especially between Christianity and Buddhism, for his promotion of the spiritual practice of gratefulness, and for his efforts to revitalize contemplative prayer life. For decades Brother David has divided his time between periods of the hermit's life and extensive lecture and retreat tours on five continents. He is the cofounder of A Network for Grateful Living (www.gratefulness.org), an organization dedicated to gratefulness as a transformative influence for individuals and society.

Brother David's spiritual classics *Gratefulness, the Heart of Prayer* and *A Listening Heart* have been reprinted and anthologized for more than two decades and translated into multiple languages. He also coauthored *Belonging to the Universe* (winner of the 1992 American Book Award), a dialogue on new-paradigm thinking in science and theology with the physicist Fritjof Capra, and his dialogue with Buddhists produced *The Ground We Share: Buddhist and Christian Practice*, coauthored with Robert Aitken Roshi. His writing has appeared in *Encyclopedia Americana*, *The New Catholic Encyclopedia*, *New Age Journal*, *Parabola* magazine, and *The Best Spiritual Writing*. Brother David's most recent books are *The Music of Silence*, cowritten with Sharon Lebell, and *Words of Common Sense*. Audio and video recordings of Brother David can be found at www.gratefulness.org.